THE SMALL BUSINESS DISASTER SURVIVAL GUIDE

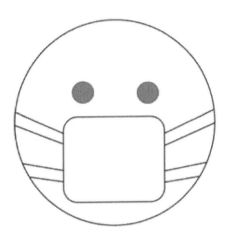

Business Continuation in
the Age of Covid-19

PHILLIP ZAGOTTI
EFFROSSINI SIMPSON
MARY BRANNON

THE SMALL BUSINESS DISASTER SURVIVAL GUIDE

Business Continuation in
the Age of Covid-19

SMALL BUSINESS DISASTER SURVIVAL GUIDE

Copyright © 2020 by Phillip Zagotti, Effrossini Simpson and Mary Brannon.
4

All rights reserved. Printed in the United States of America. No part of this book may be used or reproduced in any manner whatsoever without written permission except in the case of brief quotations embodied in critical articles or reviews.

The publishers and authors of this book have used their best efforts to prepare this work and make no representation or warranties as to its accuracy, completeness, and specifically disclaim all warranties including without limitation any implied warranties of merchantability or fitness for a particular use. The fact that an organization, website, or product is referred to in this work as a citation or potential source of further information does not mean that the publisher or author endorses the information, goods, or services sold by that company. This publication is sold with the understanding that the publisher and authors are not engaged in the rendering of professional services. The advice and strategies contained herein may not be suitable for your situation. Therefore, you should consult with a specialist where appropriate. Further, the reader should be aware that websites listed in this work may have changed or disappeared between the time this book was writing, and the time it was read. Neither the publisher nor the author shall be liable for any loss of profit or any other commercial damages, including but not limited to special damages, incidental damages, consequential damages, or other damages.

For information contact :

(Address, website)

http://www.website.com

Book and Cover design by Designer
ISBN: 9798641169859

First Edition: April 2020

10 9 8 7 6 5 4 3 2 1

This book is dedicated to those who have the strength to pursue their dreams and take the chances necessary to achieve them.
- Phillip Zagotti

This book is also dedicated to those who will face adversity during this time, but will grow from it.
- Effrossini Simpson

Dedicated to those who instead of waiting for a seat at the table, decide to build their own.
- Mary Brannon

Table of Contents

INTRODUCTION	Page 1
THE PLAYBOOK	Page 4
LOANS & FUNDING	Page 23
EMPLOYMENT ISSUES	Page 45
INSURANCE	Page 67
CONTRACTS	Page 77
BANKRUPTCY	Page 89
NONPROFITS	Page 103

CHAPTER ONE

INTRODUCTION

Business continuation is concerned with how a business can survive in a disaster or economic shock. These issues are routinely addressed by larger companies with operations in regions that commonly experience hurricanes, tornados, floods, and earthquakes. However, companies that operate in other, less disaster-prone areas of the country are not as likely to have a business continuation plan in place. For instance, New York City, is not known for routinely facing natural disasters. As a result, many companies did not have business continuation plans in place when the 9/11 attacks destroyed the World Trade Center. According to Investopedia, roughly 18,000 small businesses closed, resulting from the destruction of the buildings and damage to other areas of lower Manhattan. Since then, many larger companies have decentralized their core business functions to different locations throughout the U.S. to reduce the risk of one single disaster shutting down the entire company. However, most small businesses have never planned for emergencies or economic shocks. As a result of the COVID-19 outbreak, most business owners are now faced with these critical questions in a real-time, rapidly changing, emotionally charged situation. These situations are not conducive for the business owner to make optimal business decisions.

This book was written to help business owners make better decisions in times of crisis. The goal of this book is to provide the small business owner with the necessary knowledge needed to quickly formulate a plan to address issues they might face in a disaster or economic shock, and in the process, limit the damage to the business, employees, vendors, and customers upon whom the company relies.

Timing

Every disaster is different. Therefore, the effects will vary based on the region's political climate and economic environment. This iteration of the book is in response to the coronavirus outbreak that is currently affecting small businesses throughout the world. This book is being completed at a time in which governments are still planning their responses to the epidemic, and the length of the epidemic is unknown. However, the general policy response to the outbreak is known, and while a few details may change over the ensuing months, the majority of fundamental issues facing small businesses will likely not be materially affected. As a result, while we discuss recently passed federal legislation, it is essential to verify that other measures have not been adopted between the publication of this book and when it is being read.

Disclaimers

This book is intended to assist small business owners with issues they may likely face after a natural disaster, outbreak, or other events that cause an unexpected economic shock. To that end, this book touches on some aspects of law, business, taxation, and economics. Because laws and taxes differ from state to state, we limit these discussions to general information. It is important to remember that issues revolving around legal issues and tax laws are factually driven and must be construed to your specific facts and circumstances. As a result, should you need the help of a lawyer or CPA, please engage such a professional in your local community.

CHAPTER TWO
THE PLAYBOOK

We do not know how long this outbreak will last. As of the writing of this book, some experts state that this outbreak could go on for months while others predict years. What we do know is business models that have existed for decades will need modifications to be effective during this period. While the expected loss of life cannot be ignored, for many companies, this is a time were a fast adaptation to new social norms could make the difference between the long-term success or failure of the company.

     Entrepreneurs are people who search for products or services that are not adequately meeting the expectation or needs of the consumer. Once the entrepreneur identifies these products or services, they find a way to satisfy the consumer efficiently and then compete with existing companies to take market share. At this moment, consumers' needs and tastes have changed, and the smart entrepreneur will see this as an opportunity to differentiate their offering and take competitor's clients. For most existing companies, these changes will require discarding this year's budgets and their multiyear business plan to taking bold steps now.

The business owner should now assemble two different business plans. The first plan is to keep the company afloat during the outbreak. The structure of this plan will depend on the type of business in question. Under these circumstances, there are three types of companies. The first type of business is not affected by the epidemic. The second are businesses affected by the outbreak who can adjust their offerings and remain operational. For this group, adjusting now is critical to retaining their customers and possibly grow their client base. The third type of business is significantly affected by the outbreak and operates in an industry that is not amenable to adaptation. For this third category, the best course of action may be to pause the business, conserve cash, possibly apply for loans and focus on plans for reopening after the quarantine is lifted.

The second business plan consists of operational and marketing strategies for the second and third types of businesses discussed above. This plan is to be implemented immediately after the quarantine restrictions are lifted. Because of the incredible speed in which these events are happening, care should be taken to thoroughly think through the second stage of this year's business plan as the economic upswing could be sudden as well.

The following are some basic action steps the business owner should take to reorient their business based on the current situation, and the customer's new needs and taste.

Communication

Irrespective of one's position in a company, currently, everyone is living through the same events. Employees have uncertainty and likely fear of what might happen to them or the company in the coming weeks or months. Fear and doubt are the enemies of a productive, healthy workforce. The business owner has a responsibility to take the lead and communicate with their employees, customers, vendors, and other stakeholders. When possible, communication should be positive, factual, and not dishonest. Statements that cultivate worry or panic are not conducive to healthy company culture. As a result, the constant communication of adverse facts already known to the recipients is counterproductive. Attempts should be made to focus on positive facts without being misleading.

Being a Leader

Business owners are expected to be leaders. However, some business owners are introverts or do not respond well under pressure. Irrespective of their comfort level, the business owner is required to take a stand and make decisions. Leadership does not just pertain to issues related to employees, customers, and vendors of the business; it also requires being a leader in the local business community.

At present, others are attempting to influence the narrative. For instance, while most banks have publicly announced ceasing foreclosure activities, other banks were late to make such announcements. Some banks and politicians used these slower media releases to criticize these banks, which resulted in reputational damage. As the outbreak continues, politicians attempt to mold the narrative to redirect blame and force larger companies to modify their manufacturing or distribution efforts. The best way to avoid this outcome is to control the narrative from the start and, where possible, prevent others from defining a business or industry in a negative light. The business owner has to be proactive by envisioning possible scenarios in which aspersions might be cast on their business. By establishing their voice in the community, the business owner can develop the public goodwill needed to carry their company through the outbreak. Additionally, this goodwill can be leveraged in the future to grow the company after normalcy is reestablished.

Employees Have Good Ideas

Often business questions are not complicated but rather merely not apparent. Therefore fresh perspectives from knowledgeable employees can often result in great solutions.

Good leaders develop relationships with their employees and should have enough confidence in these relationships to approach their employees and crowdsource ideas regularly. Many times, business owners and managers are surprised by the knowledge and insight their employees have on various business matters. This should not come as a shock because these employees may have spent years working for the company and have observed aspects of the company that might not be apparent to others. In other words, perspective matters, and employees will have different insights based on their job function and prior experience.

Additionally, crowdsourcing ideas develop employee engagement and generally result in higher levels of buy-in. Even when alternative options are chosen, the employees know that their opinions were heard, and they had a seat at the table. Over time this practice can lead to a healthier, more open relationship between the business owner and their employees.

Marketing

Because of the extended timeframe of this economic disruption, many companies will not be able to save their way out of this problem. Rather businesses will have to find ways to sell their goods and services under these new circumstances. While some business owners may feel guilty about selling under these circumstances, so long as they are selling a legitimate product or service that the public wants at a fair price, such concerns are unfounded. By operating an honest business that provides income and jobs, the business owner is playing an essential part in their community's fight to overcome the adverse effects of this outbreak.

However, care should be taken to avoid negative publicity. For instance, most states implemented restrictions limiting on-site work to those who are deemed essential based on the industry or function. In the process, many business owners running nonessential businesses like flooring and furniture stores remain open and require their employees to be present or lose their job. Such actions are understandable because business owners are under extreme financial stress and facing potential financial ruin. But if the business owner continues public operations of a nonessential business and an employee or a customer contracts COVID-19 and dies, the company and its owner could face severe media scrutiny. This threat also exists for those companies that claim to "technically" be an essential business. Society does not judge people based on the technical reading of the law but instead asks if the business owner's actions were in line with the community's social morals and values. Therefore business owners should consider the potential risks in ignoring the state-mandated orders.

While some companies will take a defensive posture and wait for these events to pass, smart companies are increasing their advertising spend and adjusting their value proposition to reflect the community's new requirements. Here, it is not enough to just market more, but rather to communicate the changes the business has made to the product, service, pricing, or even delivery method to make consumers aware of the options they now have. Additionally, marketing that communicates a sense of commitment to the customer and the community is appropriate at this time. Because this kind of marketing requires a different tone existing marketing campaigns will likely need to be adjusted immediately. In the process, the company will retain current clients and could gain new clients while building goodwill that will far outlast this outbreak.

Rethinking the Business Model

The speed of change has been ever-increasing, but companies have grown accustomed to managing the change in a planned, systematic manner. Unfortunately, for most businesses, intended, systematic change is not an option for the immediate future. A lot of the old playbook that was carefully constructed over decades of experience is not currently relevant. As a result, the old systems and procedures may need to be broken in an unplanned fashion to adapt quickly. This will be especially difficult for larger companies that have employees entrenched in routine practices and standards. Here, the unorthodox thinkers within the company should be encouraged to speak up and communicate their opinions.

The outbreak represents a threat or an opportunity depending on the business and its leadership. Companies will creatively find ways to adjust their service offerings, or they will wait for this outbreak to pass and hope that they do not run out of cash in the process. What these companies may not realize is that their competition is currently making changes and advertising these changes to the public. So, while a company may be able to ride-out this epidemic, they may lose customers, which may result in a smaller, less profitable company in the future. In other words, now is the time to be brave and innovative with an eye to pragmatism.

For most companies, the question, for now, is how to deliver goods and services with as little direct contact as possible. Consumer taste for such arrangements has gained popularity over the past decade.

Source: The U.S. Census Bureau

According to the U.S. Census Bureau, in 2010, online sales only accounted for roughly 4.5% of all retail sales in the U.S. By 2019, that percentage has grown to over 10%. With the emergence of the coronavirus, consumers' preference for online consumption with little to no human interaction will continue to gain in popularity.

    While people report that they enjoy the convenience of being able to shop from their phone or computer and not being limited to the stock selection at one particular store, some shoppers still prefer the shopping experience. For these consumers, the store atmosphere and the experience of the excursion is a value to the shopper. As a result, some companies have made personal service and store atmosphere a feature that differentiates them from their competitors. Unfortunately, this feature will be of less value to consumers over the next few months. However, companies that have pursued this strategy could still market a high level of personal service, but the interactions with the clients will, for the moment, be primarily online. If this outbreak is short-lived, then consumers will be able to resume their consumption patterns with little change, and companies that offer higher levels of personal service and atmosphere will be able to continue to pursue this strategy. But, if this outbreak extends over an extended period, consumers may become comfortable with online methods of shopping, and the demand for the shopping experience may be irrevocably diminished.

That said, it is essential to remember that people still need goods and services. Appliances will break; homes will need repair; cars will need oil changes/inspections, and teeth will require cleaning. Consumptions of products and services will not completely stop as a result of the outbreak. Therefore, companies will always have an opportunity to provide services and goods at a profit.

Spending

As the coronavirus has caused fear and economic disruption, the actual economic and social effects have not yet been felt for many businesses. Shopping malls and restaurants are reporting slowing activity as people opt to stay home, away from crowds. For small businesses, these trends are alarming because, as business and the economy slows, financial challenges result. As companies identify signs of this slowdown, tough decisions will immediately be confronted. Many companies could soon face the prospect of laying off or reducing the work hours of valued employees or be unable to pay their bills as they come due over the next few months.

As the business starts to slow, decisive action must be taken immediately to preserve the company's cash and assets. Unfortunately, many owners wait longer than they should to adjust staffing levels to the company's new needs. In the process, the owners expend a lot of cash that might be needed to sustain the company over the next few months or years. While we go into further detail about staff layoffs and other workforce adjustment alternatives later in this book, one piece of advice that cannot be overstated is the need to have a plan. Decide at what point layoffs will happen and who will be chosen. By doing this, the business owner takes the emotion out of the action and is more likely to trigger staff changes promptly.

On the revenue side, businesses that carry high levels of customer receivables could realize a slowdown in their collections due to the outbreak. As a result, small companies need to be alert for signs of credit or financial weakness in their customers and take appropriate actions to reduce credit risk. This may require that the business owner take actions that jeopardize existing business relationships. However, as already discussed above, not all businesses will be proactive in their management of this outbreak and may cause financial damage to their creditors.

On the spending side, when a business runs out of cash, it is bankrupt. In times of economic stress, it is essential to the survival of most small businesses to try and retain money for extended periods. To do this, companies should look at working with suppliers to extended credit terms from the traditional 30 days to 60 or 90 days. Additionally, renegotiating pricing in contracts with suppliers and property leases is advisable. Unfortunately, suppliers will also be experiencing their own financial stresses at the same time the company is attempting to renegotiate the terms of an existing contract. As a result, some suppliers may not be able to give any concessions. For instance, because of the disruptions in the international supply chain that has occurred due to China and Germany being taken offline for some time, a company's suppliers may be facing significant cost increases or even a shortage of needed supplies over the next few months. Therefore, business owners should be prepared for contracts to be breached and to, were necessary, breach existing contracts, and find other cost-efficient sources of needed supplies to keep the company operational while conserving cash. Later in this book, we discuss general contract issues that might result from this slowdown and what the business owner should be aware of when they or their client breach a contract.

Further, businesses may have a need to find outside sources of cash in order to survive the economic shock. Unfortunately, most small businesses have not built a credit history. As a result, it will likely be up to the business owner to use their personal credit to establish a lending vehicle to acquire the needed cash. What cannot be stressed enough is the need to develop a connection with a banker immediately and, to the extent possible, explore various credit vehicles that might be available. The good news is that interest rates have never been lower, and the federal government has earmarked billions to make small business loans and grants. But other companies will be pursuing these same sources of funds, so being proactive in asserting the need for cash and accurately projecting cash shortages is vitally important.

Company Management

If the outbreak does cause significant financial difficulty to a company, it will be the responsibility of the directors and officers to take reasonable actions to protect the shareholders and company from financial harm. This may require directors to look at financial and operational moves in a concise time frame. Because officers and directors have a duty to avail themselves of the knowledge reasonably needed to make an informed decision, directors should not sacrifice proper due diligence for the sake of speed. This means that directors and officers need to be prepared to spend significantly more time attending to corporate matters.

    For corporations to make official decisions, there must generally be a board of directors meeting. Official decisions cannot be made without the minimum number of directors needed to make a quorum. If travel becomes impossible during the outbreak, in-person board meetings may become difficult for those who do not reside locally. Therefore the board may not be able to form a quorum. Consequently, boards may be precluded from making important decisions promptly. This may also lead to decisions being made outside of the formal channels prescribed by the companies operating agreement. Thus, the directors should review the business operating agreement to ascertain if a board meeting can be held through video or telecommunication devices. If the operating agreement does not allow for remote board meetings, it might be advisable to investigate what steps can be taken to allow such meetings.

Materially Adverse Events

Materially adverse events are developments, conditions, or events that would reasonably be expected to have an adverse material effect on a business's operations or financial condition. When such circumstances occur, the company is required to restate public financial statements to reflect the changed circumstances. Materially adverse events do not generally include worsening economic / market conditions or national disasters. This exclusion only applies to the extent that the effects on the company are not disproportional to others in the same industry. If the outbreak worsens and companies choose not to restate projected financials or do not publicly disclose material information, the company may run the risk of shareholder suits as well as state and federal securities actions. Additionally, materially adverse event language may exist in merger and acquisition agreements as well as debt instruments, and trigger a requirement to disclose, and potentially even an opportunity for other parties to exit the agreement.

Remote Work Considerations

The push to remote work capability or telecommuting has been a goal for many companies before the outbreak started. For many professional firms, remote capabilities have been a necessity as their employees spend a significant amount of time traveling. However, smaller businesses may not have needed to develop a remote work capability and now find themselves having to establish that capability quickly. For many smaller companies that do not use custom software installed on a central server pivoting to a remote work environment can be quick and cheap. Free software like Facebook Messenger, Google Hangout, Signal, and Telegram allow people to send text, make calls, and even video chat with little effort and at no cost. Filing sharing software like Box, Dropbox, or Google Docs is very inexpensive and easy to install. While this may not be the optimal arrangement under the circumstances, most small businesses can implement these solutions to stay somewhat functional in a remote work environment.

Security Issues

Cybersecurity should be a significant concern for any business that stores client data. Companies that have a central server and only allow their employees to work from the office have a lower risk of experiencing a data breach. In the process of establishing a remote work environment, the chances for data loss increase. But there are a few safeguards that can be taken to reduce the chances of a data breach. Below is a discussion of some general cybersecurity practices to help prevent a data breach. However, please be aware that different industries have specific standards that may need to be considered when establishing a remote work environment.

     First, the business should control who has access to data. All the filing sharing programs discussed above can limit a user's access to specific folders. For most of the programs, access can be given and retracted within a few clicks. Business owners should use this function to restrict access to information to only those employees who need to access it.

Unfortunately, many data breaches are the result of a disgruntled employee who had access to data and decided to use it for nefarious purposes. As companies may be making staffing adjustments in the near future, it is essential to delete employees' access to company data immediately before they are let go.

Second, people without direct access to information can still gain access to information through social engineering, which is the process of gaining someone's trust and tricking them into providing information or access to information. Avoiding this security breach requires establishing procedures and employee training. Because ex-employees will have already established relationships of trust with coworkers, the dismissed employee should be removed from messaging groups, and emails. The business may even want to announce the exit of the dismissed employee so that the remaining employees are not tricked into providing the employee with data or other information they should not have.

Third, passwords are essential, and while none of us like to reset them every 90 days, establishing and changing complex passwords is a valuable information safeguard. Businesses who are quickly pivoting to a virtual office environment will be implementing a lot of new software packages in a concise timeframe. In the process, it is essential to remember to establish proper password requirements to restrict access to data and other company communications.

Forth, various employees may be using different means to connect to the internet. As a result, data security will be affected by your employee's home Wi-Fi settings and other security issues. The easiest way to mitigate these issues is to require the employee to only use the company computer while performing their job. Installing a Virtual Private Networking (VPN) software on the work computer can help to keep connections between the work computer secure. VPN software is cheap to purchase and install.

Finally, this outbreak will dissipate over time, and while some companies may find a remote work environment beneficial to the company and its employee's many businesses will want to return to the work patterns established before the outbreak. In doing so, the company should take care to migrate newly created data and files back to their old systems and permanently delete the files from any temporarily established file-sharing software. Along the same lines, care should be taken to permanently delete any messaging groups formed during the remote work period as information discussed and files shared through the messaging apps could represent security risks in the future.

The Grand Reopening

Over time state-mandated quarantine restrictions will end. As businesses reopen and the economy starts to thaw, strategic decisions need to be made. The business owner needs to consider how to modify the company and its operations based on the client's new tastes. For instance, clients may now be averse to touching doors or holding menus. Therefore the business owner may want to consider automatic doors, allowing touchless entry into the building. Additionally, restaurants may want to have a Quick Response (QR) code visible in various parts of the restaurant to enable customers to use their cellphone to look at the menu. This solution has an added benefit as the restaurant will reduce printing costs while being able to adjust menu offerings and pricing quickly.

The grand reopening also requires the business owner to examine staffing needs. If the business has laid off employees, will they be able to rehire them? The CARES Act has added an extra $600 a week to the state unemployment benefits. As a result, employees may receive more money through unemployment than as an employee. Here the employer will either raise wages to encourage people to come back to work or provide other incentives. As will be discussed in chapter four, rehired employees may be eligible for expanded benefits. However, the company may qualify for the Employment Retention Credit, which could offset those benefits expenses.

Finally, the business owner needs to consider the changes they want to retain. For example, now that work from home has proven effective, can the company allow some employees to work remotely? This option could result in happier employees who view work from home options as a benefit while enabling companies to reduce expenses. Another hot topic is business travel. The quarantine has demonstrated the power and effectiveness of video communications as a substitute. While some business travel will still be required, many clients may be happier with frequent video calls. In addition, if COVID-19 remains a potential threat, travel will pose a danger to businesses and their employees.

CHAPTER THREE

LOAN AND OTHER FUNDING SOURCES

Most larger companies will be able to endure the effects of economic shock and last for significant periods with little cash flow. This is because larger companies have access to the equity and debt markets, which gives them the needed liquidity to withstand short term economic stresses. For example, Boeing has stayed operational even though its new 737-Max airliners have been grounded due to safety issues. While this has significantly hindered their cash flows and caused enormous expense to Boeing, the company is still operational and is expected to survive the manufacturing flaw. One of the reasons Boeing was able to survive is because the company sold $3.5 billion in bonds to the debt market to stay liquid.

While most small businesses do not have access to the credit markets, they should have a relationship with their local banker. These small business bankers can guide business owners through the web of paperwork needed to apply for loans, set up a line of credit, or factor receivables. Regardless of the type of loan in question, the bank will want a current set of financial statements for the business for the previous three years as well as the company's (and potentially the owner's) federal and state income tax returns.

The discussion below looks at some of the more popular loans available to companies with an eye towards current SBA loan programs and other financial assistance recently passed by the federal government. Based on the size of the economic shock and the amount of interest small businesses have in acquiring these loans, the loan packages passed by congress are likely not adequate to cover the needs of the small business community. Therefore, the reader should not assume that the SBA and government funding programs discussed below are still available.

Because no two businesses are the same, we cannot give guidance as to which option is right under your circumstances. In some situations, the optimal solution may be a combination of the various options discussed below.

Line of Credit

A line of credit ("LOC") is one of the most useful loans for a small business. It is a credit facility that every small business owner should always have available because it protects the company from economic shock by providing liquidity when there is an interruption in business or cashflows. These loans are intended to provide cash for the business to cover the operating cost and acquire inventory and act as a credit card account in that it is designed to be a short-term loan. But unlike credit cards, they have significantly lower interest rates. Further, these debt facilities are not intended to be used to purchase real estate or other equipment. In some situations, the bank will require the business to secure the LOC with outstanding accounts receivable or other assets to help ensure debt repayment.

Credit Card Financing

Some small business owners may have to turn to credit cards to keep the business operational during an economic shock. This is especially true when the economic collapse is sudden, and there is little time to get to a bank or when the trauma affects the banks' ability to make loans. While some companies have tried to build their company's credit, many small business owners have not had the opportunity to establish their company's credit history. When needed, the business owner uses their personal credit to fund noncash purchases.

For those business owners who will have to use their personal credit, they need to remember that they are individually responsible for the credit card charges irrespective of the survival of the business. Additionally, accumulating large credit card balances will reduce the person's credit score. This may become an issue if the business owner has to search out new lines of credit to keep the company operational.

It should go without saying that the credit card option is the most expensive form of financing covered in this section. The business owner should make sure that the business will be able to generate enough income after the economic shock has passed to pay the principal and interest payments on the credit cards as they become due.

If the business owner is forced to use their credit cards to float the business for a period, there are things that the business owner can do to minimize the damage. First, the business owner should try to have at least three different cards with significant limits and try not to use a considerable percentage of their available credit. Second, having three or more cards will give the business owner options if the bank or financial institution cancels one of their cards. Finally, if the business owner has to rely on their credit cards, they should look for lower interest "teaser" rates to shift existing credit card balances to save on the interest charges and pay down the debt quicker.

Factoring

Factoring receivables is a form of financing in which the business technically sells its receivables to a finance company in return for cash. Generally, the business will only receive roughly 80% of the value of the receivables at the time of the sale but will receive the remaining 20% minus fees and charges when the business's customer pays the outstanding receivable in full. The downside of this arrangement is that the fees can be costly and, if the client does not pay their debts, the factoring company can force the business to repurchase the debt.

The U.S. Small Business Administration

President Trump pushed for fiscal stimulus, including a program for small business loans to lessen the effects of the coronavirus on small businesses. This program is managed through the U.S. Small Business Administration ("SBA"). Among other things, the SBA offers disaster assistance loans at low-interest rates to businesses. After most significant natural disasters, the SBA processes loans to help people rebuild their homes and businesses in an attempt to get communities back on their feet. Most people think of these loans in relation to physical damage to homes and businesses as a result of a natural disaster. But the SBA can also give loans based on economic injury. Unfortunately, this means that newer companies without a prior business history will have a hard time pursuing an SBA loan based on economic injury. However, the SBA does offer new business loans that may still be an option for some newer small businesses, and some loans passed in response to the current outbreak only require the business to be in existence as of February 15, 2020.

Economic Injury Disaster Loan Program

For the coronavirus outbreak, the SBA has been given the authorization to make up to $120 billion in loans and grants to businesses and individuals. The SBA has set up an Economic Injury Disaster Loan Program (EIDL) in which it can make up to $2 million in loans to pay the debts, payroll, and accounts payable expenses that cannot be paid out of profits due to the impact of the coronavirus. The interest rate for the EIDL is 3.75% for small businesses and 2.75% for nonprofits with a repayment period of up to 30 years. The terms of each loan will be determined on a case-by-case basis.

To be eligible, the governor of the state in which the small business operates must have made an application to request EIDL assistance. The program will further be limited to specific designated affected communities within the state. The designated counties in which the loans will be available are listed on the SBA's website. Because these events are still unfolding, new counties will likely be added to the SBA's list as time goes on. But as stated above, even if your county does not appear on the SBA's designated county list, the other small business loan options may still be available.

The CARE Act provided an additional $10 billion to make immediate advanced payments to eligible companies. When the company makes an application under this program, they can request an advance up to $10,000 to cover payroll costs and other expenses while their loan application is being processed. The advance does not have to be repaid even if the loan request is denied. This program requires the SBA to fund the request within three days, but the SBA will predetermine the company's eligibility before distributing the advance payment.

While the original bill gives most readers the impression that the loan amount could be up to $10,000 based on the applicant's request, the SBA has provided further guidance by announcing that they are giving $1,000 per person employed by the business up to

$10,000. This position presents a problem because only 19% of small businesses in the U.S. have employees, with the other 81% being solos and contractors. The SBA's policy to limit 81% of the small business population to only $1,000 effectively prevents meaningful assistance from getting to the small businesses.

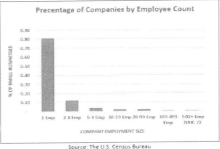

Once an advance is approved, the SBA communicates the recipient and the amount of advance to the U.S. Treasury, who will later distribute the funds. Eligibility is based on the applicant's sworn application, which is made under penalty of perjury. Therefore, the applicant should take care to fully and honestly complete the application.

The CARE Act also modified the guarantee requirements for the Economic Injury Loan program. Now the SBA can waive the personal guarantee requirement for loans under $200,000 and advance payments.

Coronavirus Aid, Relief and Economic Security

Coronavirus Aid, Relief and Economic Security (CARES) Act includes financial incentives and tax relief to businesses, workers, and families affected by the outbreak. Because this legislation is rather large, we will keep the analysis to crucial provisions that would be relevant to business owners.

- **Small Business Interruption Loans – Paycheck Protection Program**. The Paycheck Protection

Program (PPP) is an SBA loan program intended to incentivize small and midsize businesses to retain employees and prevent layoffs by making a loan that the government will later forgive if the funds are spent per the program's requirements. The loan amount is calculated by taking the companies' average monthly payroll for wages and benefits for all employees earning less than $100K, existing mortgage interest expense, rent, and utilities cost for the last 12 months and multiplying them by 2.5. The recipient company then has eight weeks after receipt of the money to cover the payroll cost, mortgage interest, rent, and utility cost. The repayment period for this loan can be up to 2 years with an interest rate of 1%. Additionally, repayment can be delayed for 6 to 12 months.

To be eligible, the business must have been in operation as of February 15, 2020, and have 500 or fewer employees who will be employed throughout the eight weeks. Independent contractors, sole proprietors, and businesses that operate in the accommodations and food service industry are also eligible to apply for the PPP. This means that larger restaurants and hotels generally not considered small businesses may also apply for these loans. Solos and contractors will have to provide documentation proving their self-employed status and make a certification that the loan is necessary to ensure continuing operations and that the funds will be used for the limited purposes under the PPP. Further, the recipient will also have to affirm that they have not made another loan application for the same purpose or have / will receive duplicative amounts through the PPP. Eligible employees are limited to no more than $100,000 annually.

The loan cannot be used for executive bonuses or stock buybacks. Staff reductions will reduce any loan forgiveness during the eight week period as compared to either the period from February 15, 2019, to June 30, 2019, or January 1, 2020, to February 26, 2020. Here the employer can choose which period to use. The loan forgiveness can also be reduced if the employer reduces pay for any employee, over 25% of their salary during the period starting February 15, 2020, and ending on April 26, 2020. But companies can rehire their previously laid-off employees to avoid this penalty. However, as discussed below, rehiring employees may result in them being immediately eligible for medical leave. Additionally, laid-off employees may receive more in unemployment benefits than working for the company. Therefore, it may be difficult for the company to convince the ex-employee to accept the new job offer. As a result, the company may not be able to achieve complete loan forgiveness.

The PPP program is not available if taken in conjunction with other SBA loan programs. However, companies with existing SBA loans can get their principal and interest payments waived for six months. Alternatively, business owners who had already acquired another SBA loan before the CARE Act was passed could apply for this loan and roll the preexisting loan into the PPP program.

Because congress envisioned this program to help small businesses, there is a requirement that a business's employee count be calculated on a consolidated basis. This means that subsidiaries cannot individually apply for this loan under the CARE Act unless all the other related entities have 500 or fewer employees in the aggregate. The aggregation requirement could be an issue for private equity and venture capital development companies because historically, the SBA has subjected these companies to affiliation rules and required aggregation. Additionally, the SBA can find an affiliation between businesses when both businesses are owned by close relatives (parents, siblings, children, spouses) and operate in the same geographic area. If the SBA finds that an affiliation exists due to the existence of a familial relationship, the applicant has the opportunity to rebut the SBA's determination with evidence to show that the business interest is separate.

The CARE Act required the SBA to process the loan application within 15 days of receiving the loan package. However, the CARE Act categorized these loan programs as a 7(a) loan, which means that the loan application will have to go through a bank. As a result, a business owner should expect the process to take 3 to 5 weeks.

While the program is intended to be an incentive program, recipients have to make a loan application. But, unlike traditional loans, this program will require the employer to provide a second request to have the loan forgiven after the employee retention period has passed. This will require the employer to keep the necessary records and submit those records as part of the loan forgiveness application process. As a result, the business owner should take great care to understand what documentation will be needed when making the loan forgiveness application. Further, the business may want to adjust their record-keeping and reporting to monitor compliance with the PPP and maximize the amount of loan forgiveness at the end of the period.

The business owner needs to remember that this program does not fully forgive the actual cost of keeping the employees on staff for the eight weeks. Instead, the loan forgiveness only applies to eight weeks based on the last 12 months' of payroll expenses, rent, and mortgage expenses. Therefore, the employer should consider this program as a discount on their labor cost over the next few months rather than free labor. But if the company is in a state of suspension as many retailers and gyms currently are, the requirement to retain employees will require cash outlays that the company, even with the PPP discount, may not be able to afford.

Because the PPP cannot be taken in conjunction with the EIDL, the business owners will need to need to look at their payroll, mortgage interest, rent, and utilities cost to see which loan provides the best benefit. Because the EIDL provides up to a $10,000 advance that does not require repayment, we would need a situation in which the PPP program would provide a better benefit. To do this, the business owner would want the PPP to result in a grant of more than the EIDL advancement. Because the PPP uses a multiple of 2.5 times the average monthly expense, we would simply divide 2.5 by $10,000 (assuming the company can get the full $10K) to arrive at the average monthly allowable cost of $4,000 or $48,000 by multiplying by 12 months. So, for businesses that have yearly payroll, mortgage interest, rent, and utility costs over $48,000, the PPP will provide a more significant benefit. However, companies coming in below $48,000 will get a more substantial benefit by pursuing the EIDL. If the yearly expense is slightly more than $48,000, the business owner may still want to pursue the EIDL because the application paperwork is simpler to complete, and the money is funded in only a few days.

- **Modifications to the Net Operating Loss Rules.** Under the Tax Cuts and Jobs Act of 2017, businesses were no longer allowed to carry their current year's losses back to previous years to use against prior reported income. It further limited the use of net operating losses (NOL) to 80% of the company's taxable income. Under the CARES Act, companies will now be able to carry NOLs from 2018, 2019, and 2020 back five years and can use losses up to 100% of that year's taxable income. This could result in some companies with high net profits in a prior year being able to amend their previous year's returns and obtain a tax refund based on last year's tax payments. Here the business owner will need to look at their prior returns to see if they made a profit in any of the preceding years and if the amount of taxes paid in the previous tax periods are substantial enough to warrant the time and expense of carrying the current losses back and amending the return.

    For business owners who decide to sell their business, these tax law changes may increase the market value of the company. NOLs sit on the balance sheet of some companies and are an asset that can transfer to the new owners. Because these NOLs can now be carried back at 100% of the taxable income, the acquiring company can recognize immediate benefits from the acquisition. As a result, if the business owner decides to place the business on the market, they need to understand how those NOLs may be of value to the right purchaser and then market the company accordingly.

- **Employee Retention Credit.** The CARES Act allows for a refundable tax credit based on 50% of the "qualified wages" paid by an "eligible employer" during the outbreak. This credit may be applied to the employer's share of their Social Security tax liability.

	Qualified wages are wages and benefits paid to the employee during the period, as will be defined further below. For businesses with less than 100 employees, the credit will be calculated as 50% of the wages paid to employees during the applicable period. Businesses with over 100 employees can only claim the credit on employees who were paid but not of service to the company during the applicable period. However, the credit is limited to $5,000 per employee and cannot be claimed in conjunction with Payroll Protection Program or other work opportunity credit. Further, this credit cannot be taken in for family leave or sick leave under FFCRA (discussed in chapter 4).

	To qualify as an "eligible employer," the business must have been partially or fully suspended due to governmental actions limiting the company's ability to operate. The credit is limited to the first quarter after December 31, 2019, in which the company's gross receipts are less than 50% of the gross receipts from the same quarter in the previous calendar year. This period will be deemed to end on the quarter in which the company's gross receipts are equal to or greater than 80% of the same quarter in the previous calendar year.

The credit is reimbursed to the employer by allowing the employer to keep the social security payroll tax withheld from their employees. This means that the credit is only useful to the employer if they continue to be in operation and employ people after the outbreak has concluded. Therefore, business owners should not pursue this credit for the sake of saving money at the expense of the cash needed to secure the company's future. Otherwise, the company could go out of business with tax credits on its balance sheet.

Because this credit interacts with other provisions of the tax code, businesses need to be careful of potential unintended consequences. For instance, companies that use work opportunity tax credits might lose that credit when selecting the retention credit option over an SBA loan. But for businesses that predominantly have lower-income employees making less than $29,000, the credit could be a better option because the $5,000 credit would result in a better discount versus the eight weeks of work expense that would be eventually forgiven under the SBA PPP Program. Conversely, businesses that predominantly have higher earning employees may find the PPP program a better option.

- **Employer Payroll Tax Deferral.** As part of the CARE Act, companies can defer their 2020 federal payroll tax payments and pay the tax over the next two years. This means that 50% of the tax will be due in 2021, with the other half being due in 2022. So, while this is not a loan in the traditional sense, it acts as a loan in that it allows the company the ability to retain needed capital. However, care should be taken when considering this option. Under these conditions, the payroll taxes are a liability that the company and potentially it's owners will be responsible for repaying irrespective of the company's future existence. Further, while it is routine to discharge SBA loans in bankruptcy, it is difficult to discharge federal tax liabilities.

- **Retirement Account Early Distribution Penalty.** Generally, taxpayers under 59.5 who take distributions from their retirement accounts (early distributions) pay a 10% penalty in addition to income taxes. Under the CARE Act, retirement account holders who have been adversely affected by the outbreak can take a COVID-19 related distribution from their retirement account of up to $100,000 without penalty or taxes so long as they repay the distribution to their retirement account within three years from the date of withdrawing. For small business owners who have retirement account savings, this is an easy and quick funding source that can give the business the liquidity it needs to outlast the outbreak.

If repayment does not occur within the three-year window, then the taxpayer will have to pay the income taxes on the distribution but will not be levied the 10% early distribution penalty. Taxpayers who do not intend to make the repayments can report the distribution as income on their 2020 tax return. If the taxpayer's income in 2020 is suppressed due to the economic effects of the coronavirus, then this course of action might be preferred because the suppressed income will result in a lower tax rate.

To qualify, the taxpayer must have been physically or financially affected by the outbreak and make the distribution during the 2020 calendar year. In effect, most people will be able to qualify for this program.

Unemployment for Self-employed/solos, Contractor, Freelancers, and Gig Workers

Independent contractors, solos, and gig workers make up a significant portion of the U.S. workforce. Unlike employees, these workers do not get benefits and are not treated the same by states when applying for unemployment. Both the CARE Act and the Families First Coronavirus Response Act (FFCRA) have made accommodations for these workers and required the state to provide them with unemployment.

Under the CARE Act, contractor/gig workers can receive unemployment if they are diagnosed with COVID-19, have a family member with the disease, have a child that is unable to attend school due to the outbreak, or cannot get to work locations due to the quarantine. Assistance is also available if the contractor/gig worker is "partially unemployed". However, contractor/gig workers are not eligible if they are receiving benefits under the FFCRA or any state benefits.

The contractor/gig worker can receive unemployment assistance for up to 39 weeks so long as they are unemployed or unable to work. But unlike regular unemployment, contractors/gig workers are not required to seek employment while on unemployment. The CARE Act gives a $600 a week benefit in addition to any state unemployment benefits and is retroactive to January 27, 2020.

The FFCRA also provided self-employed, contractors, and gig workers paid sick leave simular to the FFCRA sick leave already discussed above. Under the FFCRA, the self-employed contractor/gig worker will need to be unable to work or telework due to quarantine as required by the government or healthcare professional, illness due to COVID-19, or to take care of a child who cannot attend school due to closure. The amount of sick leave is based on the individual's average daily income up to $511 per day for up to 10 days. If the leave is due to quarantine, self-isolation, or to care for a child, then the amount is 67% of the average daily income up to $200 per day for up to 10 days.

When calculating the daily income, the self-employed, contractors, and gig workers need to divide their income by 260 days and not 265. Unlike the CARE Act, the FFCRA is effective for events after April 1, 2020.

Self-employed, contractors, and gig workers should be on notice that applying for these benefits will require filing applications with the state. Because states benefit from contractors and gig workers being class employees, it is likely that the states will use the data they receive from the applications to target companies for employment tax audits in the future. Additionally, contractor and gig workers who have not filed state income tax returns may find themselves the target of income tax audits based on the data they file in their application. Therefore the self-employed, contractors, and gig workers should assess their options carefully based on their individual circumstances.

False Claims Act

The False Claims Act (FCA) imposes civil and criminal liability on those who make false or misleading claims to the U.S. government in an attempt to extract payments. The Department of Justice (DOJ) enforces the FCA, although other federal agencies have the authority to pursue actors as well. The CARES Act includes an oversight requirement, and the SBA and DOJ are working together to combat fraudulent applications. The DOJ has publically stated that it will make CARES Act fraud a top enforcement priority. Therefore business owners making an application for relief to any federal government agency should be careful to ensure that the representations they are making are factual and not misleading. If the applicant is later contacted by the SBA or DOJ related to the validity of information contained in the loan application, the applicant should consider contacting legal counsel to examine the potential liabilities that may exist.

Accelerating Losses to the Preceding Tax Year

When a presidentially declared natural disaster occurs, the IRS code allows companies to carry losses resulting from the disaster back to the prior tax year. This option is valuable for those businesses that have tax liabilities in 2019. By pulling applicable 2020 expenses into 2019, the company can reduce its 2019 tax liabilities and conserve cash. To be eligible, the loss must occur due to the disaster, not covered by insurance, and be entirely sustained in the tax year.

Examples of losses available for acceleration include:

1. Cost of permanently closing a business location due to COVID-19
2. Retirement of fixed assets due to COVID-19
3. Abandonment of leasehold improvements due to permanently closing a business location
4. Inventory waste expense due to government-mandated quarantine due to COVID-19

Lost revenue or decline in asset market value is generally not eligible for accelerated loss treatment.

Because these losses have to be connected to the outbreak, this tax strategy is dependant on specific facts and circumstances unique to a particular business. Therefore the business owner should seek counsel from a tax CPA or tax attorney to examine their options.

Final thoughts

Most business owners will want to know which loan program is right for them. Because each business is different, each business owner will have to analyze the facts and circumstances unique to their specific business and the market they operate in. For instance, companies attempting to retain employees may not have that option even with the PPP discount due to cash shortfalls. As an alternative, the SBA Economic Injury loan does not have an employee retention requirement and is much easier to apply for. But some companies may not have the ability to survive with the additional interest cost that comes with a larger loan. Most companies will need to put pencil to paper based on different scenarios to discern which options will be the best for them.

If the business does not have a good set of financial statements or is behind in their tax filings, it is imperative that they contact a CPA or other financial professional to get these necessary documents prepared. Because the economic shock to a small business could be abrupt and unexpected, business owners will likely have little time to react to the situation and create a set of financial statements, file unfiled tax returns and develop a relationship with their banker. Because economic shocks reverberate through different industrial sectors at different rates, companies that are not currently experiencing the effect of the outbreak may find that these effects are only delayed and not avoided. Therefore, going through these steps now and establishing a line of credit in preparation for a potential slowdown could significantly increase the chances of a small business surviving the economic effects of this pandemic.

Additionally, timing must also be considered. Merchant Maverick reports that it takes the SBA roughly 4 to 5 weeks to approve and fund an SBA disaster loan. Other traditional SBA loans can take between 2 to 4 months to support and fund. Unfortunately, many small businesses do not have the liquidity to continue to operate while they wait for the 1 to 4 months for the SBA to approve their loan. Some very efficient banks have been known to support and fund loans within three weeks, but this is not standard practice.

Finally, loan approval is not guaranteed. Banks and the SBA have lending standards. While some criteria may be relaxed as a general rule, most lending institutions expect the return of their money. Therefore, business owners who struggle to keep the door open while waiting for approval of a loan may need to consider the existing health of the company and their creditworthiness to assess the wisdom of such a plan.

CHAPTER FOUR
EMPLOYEE ISSUES

One of the most challenging things a business owner has to do is lay people off. It is neither pleasant for the employee nor the employer, but under some circumstances, layoffs must occur for the health and survival of the business. Because of the discomfort involved in layoffs, most business owners delay the act much longer then they should and, in the process, financially harm their business and company morale. Unfortunately, being a leader means having to make tough decisions and take decisive actions in times of trouble.

The Layoff

Companies approach layoffs in a variety of ways. Some may choose to lay people off on an individual basis based on performance and skills. Other companies manage layoffs based on the position and how it fits into the post-layoff company. Under a position based layoff plan, the person in the position is not relevant. As a result, companies could inadvertently keep employees who are not a good fit and, in the process, let other high performers go.

Another approach for larger companies is to require each department to reduce its headcount by a prescribed number of people. This leaves the decision of who will remain in the hands of the department heads. This is an excellent method because it uses the department manager's localized knowledge to determine who fits best in the post layoff company. However, caution should be taken to avoid favoritism in the process.

Generally, most layoffs are preceded by days, weeks, or even months of employee stress. The employees usually have a sense of the health of the company and the market in which it operates. As a result, they likely suspect changes are coming. This uncertainty and fear affect employee morale and performance. Layoffs significantly hinder the company culture for a significant period after layoffs occur. The main goal of a properly managed layoff is to minimize the damage to the company and allow the remaining staff to perform their job and reduce uncertainty effectively. To that end, a round of layoffs should happen at one time and not in a staggered or trickle process. After the layoffs have occurred, management and owners should communicate to the remaining staff that no further layoffs are planned to reduce uncertainty.

Furloughs

While most have heard about furloughs in relation to government shutdowns, furloughs are also used by businesses to control labor costs during times of seasonal shutdowns or supplier shortages that force plants to go idle. A furlough occurs when a company requires employees to take mandatory leave without pay. Under this approach, companies generally furlough some of their employees for a defined period and then reemploy them after that time has passed. During that period, some employers may still provide benefits, but the employee is not allowed to do any work for the company. The main difference between a layoff and a furlough is that employees who are furloughed have an expectation of being recalled and may receive benefits during their furlough period.

If the small business decides to pursue a furlough to adjust staffing levels for the period in question, the employer needs to remember the no-work rule, which states that no furloughed employee may perform any work for the company without pay. This means that simple tasks like forwarding an email or answering a call from a client could result in the company being liable to the furloughed employee for an entire day's pay if the employee is an exempt employee. For nonexempt employees, the payment would be based on the amount of time they worked for the company while on furlough.

State Shared Work Program

Some states offer shared work, partial unemployment programs for those who have not been laid off but have had their work hours significantly reduced. Here, employers who are reducing employee work hours allow the state to provide partial unemployment benefits to the affected employees. A significant number of states offer a shared work program. Generally, the company has to apply for the program and submit reports to the state. The state uses this information to calculate how much unemployment various employees should receive in a given period. Some states limit the amount of time an employee can work for the employer in a given week while in the program. In most cases, enrolling in a shared work program affects the company's experience rating and increases the company's unemployment tax rate in future years. But these are just general rules which can vary depending on the state. Therefore, it is essential to become familiar with the specifics of the available programs in the states your company operates.

An Alternative Method

Some companies have taken an alternative approach to layoffs by reducing wages instead of laying people off. This is especially useful for "exempt" employees who receive a salary periodically. For these employees, reducing work hours would not affect their wages and thus have no effect on company expenses. Studies on this approach have noted that high performers have a greater likelihood of leaving the company over the next six months, and overall morale is damaged. To limit the damage associated with a wage reduction plan, the company should communicate its intention to restore pay to their pre-reduction levels so that employees do not think it is permanent. But this alternative method has the positive effect of maintaining a team-based corporate culture. Additionally, when the economic shock has passed, and business starts to improve, a company that followed this plan will have trained employees ready to take on new opportunities. By contrast, their competitors will have to hire and train new staff. For those who decide to pursue this option, it is essential that the employee's hourly pay still equals or exceeds the legal minimum wage.

Hourly Employees

Generally, hourly employees are considered "nonexempt" employees, meaning they do not receive a set salary. Instead, they are paid based on the time they work during some predefined period. A business can reduce the number of hours these nonexempt employees work to control costs. But, the potential for employee attrition increases and company culture is negatively affected due to the reduced hours. However, this option is good because it allows the company to have a flexible workforce while retaining its skilled employees. As a result, the company is in a better position to grow after the economic shock passes.

If a wage reduction approach is pursued in conjunction with a PPP loan, the company should take care not to exceed the 25% wage reduction limitation. Similarly, the PPP program requires that payroll distributions be in line with the prior year's average cost. Companies that pursue a wage reduction plan could find that they are not able to spend all the money they received in the PPP loan. Additionally, wage reductions may prevent the company from achieving the 75% labor expense threshold applied by the SBA. These mistakes will result in the reduction of loan forgiveness and an added need for cash at a time when the company can ill afford to spend it. Therefore, the company may want to examine taking a smaller PPP loan to avoid these potential outcomes.

COBRA Insurance

COBRA insurance was the result of the Consolidated Omnibus Budget Reconciliation Act of 1985 (COBRA). The COBRA coverage requirements apply to an employer who has over 20 employees. Employers who do not have a COBRA compliant plan are subject to tax penalties. COBRA insurance allows employees and their immediate family members to maintain the healthcare coverage they had before a qualifying event. Qualifying events include voluntary or involuntary termination, reduction in work hours, layoffs, medical leave, or even a slowdown in business operations that affect the employee's status. Employees are allowed to maintain existing coverage at the same level. However, a separated employee is responsible for covering the expense based on the employer's cost plus a 2% administration fee. Generally,

COBRA insurance is permitted for up to 18 months. But, the COBRA insurance policy can be terminated if the separated employee does not pay or if the former employer ceases to maintain a health insurance policy.

As employers layoff, furlough, or reduce employee's work hours as a result of the financial shock caused by the coronavirus, some employees with existing health insurance coverage will become entitled to COBRA benefits. This requires the employer to notify the discharged employee of their rights to their COBRA benefits after the qualifying event and provide directions to continue coverage.

Finally, COBRA does not apply to companies that go out of business or file bankruptcy.

Retention Bonuses

Retention bonuses are payments made outside the employee's regular salary as an incentive to remain with the company. Retention bonuses are typical during mergers and acquisitions, at crucial periods during business operations, or during a time of disruption. Generally, such events might make some key employees uneasy about the company's future or cause the employee to have doubts about the existence of their position. Additionally, competitors may see this as an opportunity to take the company's key employees and gain a competitive edge.

To convince the employee to remain with the company, the employer may offer a bonus to compensate them for the risk of staying. Retention bonuses can also be used during times of layoffs to incentivize employees to remain with the company or accept a temporary pay reduction. In essence, the employer is shifting costs to a future time period following the economic shock. However, the employer should take care to structure the retention bonus so it is not due to the employee until some specified future date or an event has happened. Otherwise, the employee could see the bonus as earned incrementally, which could trigger payroll liabilities even if the employee leaves. Further, an incrementally earned bonus could result in tax issues for both the employee and the employer.

Hiring

Many businesses recruit college students in their final year of college to begin work after graduation. This is especially common in accounting and law firms for whom recruiting is essential to keeping their talent pipeline full. While many are expressing hope that the outbreak will subside by the summer, no one can guarantee any timeline. Further, companies may not need the recruited talent in the near term as economic conditions are likely to thaw out rather than instantly return to normal. As a result, companies may want to manage incoming talent. If the executed employment contract can be modified or voided, and the company does not need or cannot afford the recruit, the company should make adjustments accordingly. Rescinding employment agreements may result in tort liability, as some recruits turned down other offers to accept positions at the company. In the 2008 market upheaval, many firms extended the start dates for some recruits to avoid possible civil liability. Some companies gave stipends to entice the candidate to accept the later start date. Since recruits are likely aware the position may not exist, this strategy will probably be successful. Further, other employment opportunities have disappeared, so the recruit has limited options.

Employment Issues

Employers already exist in a minefield of state and federal employment regulations. Most business owners know the general rules concerning employee rights and the formalities of managing staff, but few have availed themselves of the potential issues that might arise with trying to manage employees during a viral outbreak. While we will attempt to cover some general labor issues small businesses may face in this critical time, it is essential to note each state has differing employment statutes that should be reviewed before taking action. One rule applicable across all states is that employers cannot enforce company policies in a discriminatory fashion. For example, employers should not prevent fathers from taking leave to care for a child due to a school closure when they allow mothers to do the same.

Families First Coronavirus Response Act

The Families First Coronavirus Response Act ("FFCRA") is a bill passed by the federal government intended to address a variety of health and employment issues stemming from the Coronavirus outbreak. Among other things, it provides for testing, a food program for children and seniors, and more money for Medicare. The bill also imposes new requirements on employers with 500 or fewer employees. The most significant change requires the employer to provide two weeks of paid sick leave for employees. This requirement applies to both full time and part-time employees regardless of how long they worked for the company. Part-time employees will receive paid leave based on the number of typical work hours. Additionally, the CARES Act (discussed previously) made a technical correction to the FFCRA that makes employees who were laid off on or after March 1, 2020, and worked for the company 30 of the last 60 days before their dismissal, eligible for leave under FFCRA when rehired. The FFCRA sick leave is in addition to the existing sick leave that the company already offers its employees.

Unlike the Family Medical Leave Act (FMLA) discussed below, the FFCRA benefits are triggered when an FMLA eligible event occurs, or the employee goes into quarantine/self-quarantine. Additionally, these benefits are available when the employee has to care for a child due to school closure, or the usual caregiver is unavailable due to the outbreak.

Employers who pay the sick leave benefits under the FFCRA are eligible for a refundable tax credit equal to 100% of the sick leave wages paid with some limitations. The primary limitation is the sick pay cannot exceed $511 a day or $200 a day if the absence was due to caring for a family member. The refund will only apply to 10 days of sick leave, and the credit is applied against the employer's social security tax liability. However, this tax credit is only available to those companies which are required to provide these benefits under FFCRA.

In addition to these new rules, the FFCRA also modifies the FMLA by making it applicable to all employees who have worked for the company for the last 30 days. The act also allows the leave to be used to care for children who cannot attend school or daycare due to closure resulting from a declaration of emergency. Similar to the FFCRA, employers who provide paid family and medical leave can get a tax credit up to $200 per day not to exceed $10,000 per employee.

While there is no express exemption to the FFCRA as there is under the FMLA, the Secretary of Labor is authorized to exempt healthcare providers and some small businesses with fewer than 50 employees if the requirements of the bill would endanger the company as a going concern. Therefore small companies potentially subject to these requirements are advised to seek counsel to examine the possibility of requesting an exemption. Additionally, small business owners should seek the counsel of a CPA to plan the proper accounting for these medical leave expenses and to timely file for the related tax credit.

The FFCRA will end on December 31, 2020, and on January 1, 2021, changes made to the Family Medical Leave Act will revert to the pre-FFCRA rules. As a result, it is advisable to review the original FMLA requirements as some small business owners may have ongoing FMLA issues that will carry over into 2021.

Unfortunately, the FFCRA is not good for employers. As will be discussed later, roughly 50% of most small businesses do not have the cash reserved needed to stay operational longer than three months. Most businesses cannot front the cash needed to cover the expanded benefits and wait three months for reimbursement. Further, federal agencies have slowed due to quarantine policies and workforce absences. As a result, it is unknown how long it will take the get an exemption from FFCRA. The result is that the FFCRA encourages businesses to layoff or furlough employees to avoid the increased cost resulting from these expanded benefits.

Family Medical Leave Act

The Family Medical Leave Act (FMLA) provides some employees up to 12 weeks of unpaid leave per year. During medical leave, the employee cannot be dismissed, and any preexisting employer-sponsored health benefits must be maintained. To qualify before the FFCRA, the employee must have worked for 12 months or at least 1,250 hours over the last 12 months for an employer with 50 or more employees within a 75-mile radius. Under the FMLA, the employee is entitled to leave to give birth, care for a newborn/adopted child, an immediate family member who is seriously ill, or health condition that prevents the employee from working. An immediate family member under the FMLA is the employee's spouse, child, or parent. However, the employee is responsible for complying with the reasonable and customary requirements of the employer for requesting medical leave.

Employees who Exhibit Signs of COVID-19 at Work

Many people live paycheck to paycheck and cannot afford to miss work. As a result, some employees will attempt to come to work while sick to avoid the loss of pay. When employees exhibit symptoms of coronavirus at work, employers can require the employee to leave. The Center for Disease Control has stated that employees with symptoms of COVID-19 should stay home. Further, the employer has a responsibility to take reasonable steps to protect their employees. By allowing an employee who presents symptoms of the virus to remain at work, the employer could become liable if other employees contract the disease.

The Americans with Disabilities Act (ADA) regulates the kinds of inquiries the employer can make about employee's medical issues. When discussing any potential health issue with an employee, the employer should be careful to limit their discussion to relevant COVID-19 related symptoms and ascertain if they can or should perform their duties. Demands that the employee takes a medical exam or inquiring as to whether they have previously visited a doctor should be approached with caution. Therefore, any investigation should be limited to COVID-19 and not delve into any unrelated issues.

Reasonable Precautions

As stated above, employers have a duty to take reasonable steps to protect their employees.

Unfortunately, reasonableness is an elusive concept because individual opinions vary. Some states have pass laws prescribing steps employers must take to protect their employees. These states now require employers to provide face masks to their employees and use them when in the public areas of the facility. Other states also require businesses to ensure customers on the premises use face masks. The Center for Disease Control (CDC) has also issued guidelines for employers that include screening employes before and during their shift, social distancing, wearing masks, and proper sanitization. While the employer may comply with these state and federally mandated standards, the employer should remember that compliance does not absolve them of civil liability. Courts judge reasonableness based on what a normal person would do in the same or similar situation. In the court's analysis, a business's compliance with the law is a factor, but it does not absolve the employer of liability when additional safeguards are necessary. Therefore employers should look to these laws as the minimum standard, they may have to exceed in some circumstances to avoid civil liability.

Require Employees to Work From Home.

To reduce personal contact with others and slow the spread of the disease, some employers may find it advantageous to have their employees work from home during the outbreak. Generally, the employer determines where and how work is performed. Assuming that the work can be performed from the employee's house, the employer can request that the employee do so. However, if the work cannot be performed at the employee's residence, and the employee is willing and able to perform their duties at the employer's location, complications may arise. Employers who restrict employees from entering the business worksite for precautionary reasons may be liable to the employee for the employee's lost pay absent exigent circumstances. Therefore, unless exigent circumstances or a government-issued quarantine order exist, the employer should be careful to document and inform the staff of the specific reason that they are forbidding employees from entering the premises.

Special Considerations for Remote Workers

When implementing a required work from home policy, the employer should take into account ADA requirements that exist for current employees. For instance, employees with existing health conditions that place them at a higher risk of contracting the illness could request to work from home as an ADA accommodation based on their preexisting condition. Further, employers are required to provide similar accommodations for disabled employees at the home office that are in line with existing workplace accommodations.

H-1B visa workers are only allowed to work at the locations listed in their Labor Condition Application (LCA). However, in national emergencies and natural disasters, state actions and employer's decisions are given great deference. As a result, if the employer has closed their offices or required the H-1B visa holder to work from home, no adverse action will likely be taken. However, if the home office is in the same Metropolitan Statistical

Area (MSA) as the employer's office, a new LCA can be posted with the home office address to cover the H-1B.

Tax issues may be another concern for some business owners. Generally, a state is entitled to tax a company when that company has some connection with that state. States typically look to where a company performs its services or sells its goods, and where company employees and assets are located. When a business has a central location at which services are performed or products sold, these issues are straightforward. However, if employees are working from home for an extended period during the outbreak and generating revenue in cities or states different from the business's offices, the company could find itself liable for payroll and income taxes in various jurisdictions. Further, the company could establish a relationship with other states sufficient enough to require the company to charge sales tax to that state's residence, which the company may not currently have a duty to do.

Most first approach this possibility with disbelief because the thought of a state using a company's actions in an emergency against them in the future to pursue tax revenue seems unjust. However, the mantra "we are all in this together" will dissipate as we move further away from the outbreak. Because this issue will likely be visited years after the epidemic has passed, such state action may not be as repugnant as it currently seems. Therefore, the business owner should verify the home addresses their employees are working from then examine the potential state tax issues that may arise.

Do I have to pay for the employees?

As already stated above, employees who live paycheck to paycheck may not want to miss work. To the extent that the company offers sick paid benefits, employees who do contract this virus should receive their sick pay benefits. Additionally, it may be in the employers' interest, if possible, to offer sick pay to any employee who contracts the virus irrespective of the status of their benefits to incentivize them to stay home and not spread the virus in the office.

While some employers may fear that some employees might take advantage of the offered benefits in an unethical manner, the benefits could be structured to allow employees who do not already receive benefits to only received a portion of their regular pay. If done correctly, this plan could result in a good balance between an employee's desire to come to work and earn an income with the incentive to avoid getting others sick.

Modernly, companies have a significant number of contract workers providing various services to the company. Because contractors do not receive benefits like employees, a reduction in work hours or temporary closure of a site could have a significant effect on a company's contract labor. If the company is the contractor's only client, then the contractor will be, for all intents and purposes, unemployed or laid off. While the CARES Act allows contractors to apply for state unemployment benefits, they may not receive the same level of benefits as an employee. Some contractors might claim they are employees to qualify for increased benefits. If the contractor makes such a claim, the company will have to defend its contractor designation.

The status of a person as a contractor versus an employee is a multifactor, fact-based inquiry, with little weight given to agreements between the contractor and company. State and federal agencies commonly reclassify people from contractor to employee. After reclassifying employees, an agency will typically back charge the company for prior taxes and workers compensation insurance. Employers should be careful not to offer benefits to contractors, as such actions will only help establish that the contractor is an employee.

Because employee-contractor issues can arise as a result of other events, companies must be proactive and review their labor classifications to avoid potential penalties.

Employee Refusing to Work

Some employees will try to avoid coming to work out of fear of contracting the virus. Under the Occupational Health and Safety Act (OHSA), employees are protected from retaliation when they refuse to work in unsafe conditions. To receive this protection, the employee must have a reason on which to base their concerns. Without such a basis, the employer may discipline the employee for not coming to work. Additionally, under the National Labor Relations Act (NLRA), employees are protected from retaliation for acting on behalf of others to improve working conditions.

Employer Reporting Requirements

OSHA places filing requirements on employers when injuries occur at their worksite. If an employee contracts coronavirus at work, OSHA would consider that a recordable illness. Further, if the employee becomes infected at work requiring hospitalization, the hospitalization will have to be reported to OSHA within 24 hours.

If a business experiences significant economic hardship due to the virus and must close a plant or lay off workers, the Worker Adjustment and Retraining Notification Act (WARN) should be considered. The WARN Act requires an employer with more than 100 employees to give a 60-day notice to employees and other stakeholders before closing a plant or laying off more than 33% of the company's workforce. However, when unforeseeable business circumstances or natural disasters necessitate the layoffs, the 60-day notice can be given after the layoffs.

Workers Compensation Insurance

During an outbreak, an employee who is affected by the virus will likely seek cash from many sources. One such source might be the employer's workers compensation insurance policy. Whether this illness is covered under workers compensation will be based on the facts surrounding the workers illness and not the disease in question.

Generally, two tests must be satisfied for a disease to qualify as an occupational illness and, therefore, covered under most workers compensation insurance policies.

First, the illness must be considered "occupational," which means it arises out of the course and scope of employment. As such, the employee must have been performing some particular activity for the employer when they were exposed. This is a fact-based analysis, but various states have interpreted this test in different ways. As a result, it is not as straightforward as one might expect. The analysis of this element is based on legal facts and not medical opinions.

Second, the illness must be caused by a condition related to the work. This element is much harder to prove because it requires the illness be found almost exclusively to workers in a particular profession or an increased exposure to the illness due to the employee's working conditions. For example, healthcare workers who contract HIV could claim workers compensation for the disease if the infection occurred on the job, as exposure to HIV is related to working in the health care profession.

Generally, the courts will look at the following facts:

1. The commonality of the illness to someone in the industry vs. the community at large.

2. The timing of the illness related to the employee's work attendance.
3. The employee's susceptibility to illness, (i.e. previous medical issues); and

4. The employee's personal activities that might have caused exposure to the illness in question.

Based on the test discussed here, the coronavirus will not result in an illness for which an employee may pursue remuneration through a worker's compensation policy. Like the flu, coronavirus spreads to others through social/community interaction and is not specific to employment. For the majority of people, contracting the illness at work, by itself, is not considered a compensable event. However, for workers in the healthcare field who are exposed to people with various diseases, including coronavirus, contracting COVID-19 may result in a compensable injury.

CHAPTER FIVE

INSURANCE

Many small businesses have a variety of insurance policies, such as liability, auto and life insurance on key employees. While most small businesses believe they have ample coverage, all too often, after a disaster, they realize their insurance policy will not cover losses. To compound matters, insurance companies will slow down the reimbursement process or attempt to deny claims. Therefore, small businesses need to be proactive and review their insurance policies to understand their coverage as it relates to this epidemic. The following is a brief overview of some insurance policies that might be relevant under the current circumstances.

Commercial General Liability Insurance

Commercial general liability insurance ("CGL") is the most common form of business insurance. CGL insurance is intended to cover losses that result from personal injury and property damage caused by a business's acts, products, or injuries that occur on the business premises. Generally, companies that open their premises to the public have a duty to warn their customers to known dangers and take reasonable steps to discover hazards that might be present. As the outbreak spreads, the business could have a duty to warn its customers and take steps to protect their customers from exposure. Retail, restaurants, entertainment, and travel-related companies could face suits from customers who contract the disease, alleging that the business did not take reasonable steps to warn them of the risk or protect them from exposure to the virus. Some companies may look to their policy to cover the cost of these claims. However, some policies explicitly exclude injuries due to illness or pollutants. Therefore, it is critical to thoroughly understand the details of your policy and evaluate the potential arguments available to overcome such policy exclusions.

Business Interruption Insurance

Business Interruption Insurance (BI) is an endorsement or add-on to the business's property insurance policy. BI policies are intended to reimburse businesses for losses of business income due to interruptions to the business's operations. This form of insurance generally covers lost revenue and payments related to fixed expenses like rent, payroll, utilities, and even costs associated with operating out of a temporary location.

Generally, this kind of insurance requires some form of physical damage to business property that prevents the business from operating at that location. However, some policies may allow for recovery due to epidemics or business interruptions that result from the actions of state or federal civil authorities. Some policies will require these civil actions to cause physical damage to the business property. For instance, during the Severe Acute Respiratory Syndrome outbreak of 2002, some companies were able to recover losses suffered as a result of disruptions to their business. After the 2002 outbreak, many insurance companies have rewritten their policies to exclude these kinds of viral epidemics. Therefore, companies must review their policies in detail to ascertain if it will cover potential losses from coronavirus.

Contingent Business Interruption Insurance

Contingent Business Interruption Insurance (CBI) is an add-on to the BI insurance policy discussed above. CBI covers losses that result from a third party on whom the business depends. When vendors or customers suffer physical damage that prevents them from fulfilling their obligations to your business and results in disruptions, the policy will reimburse the company for the economic losses. Here no direct physical damage has to occur to the company or their assets. With widespread disruptions in global supply chains as a result of the virus's effect on China, many small businesses may already have a potential claim depending on the exact wording of their policy.

Event Cancellation Insurance

Event Cancellation Insurance is generally purchased by companies that are involved in managing events, concerts, festivals, and other public gatherings. Event cancellation insurance is intended to cover lost revenue and expenses that result from postponement or cancellation of an event due to natural disasters, bad weather, terrorism, or contract breaches by event performers. Generally, these policies do not cover cancelations due to viral or bacterial outbreaks. However, if the event is canceled due to state or federal civil action, then event cancellation insurance could become available for recovery. While some events will be canceled based on the event promoter's best judgment, such circumstances by themselves do not give rise to a valid claim. Here the organizer has to cancel due to a covered event as defined in the policy, or no recovery will be granted.

Trade Credit Insurance

Trade Credit Insurance (TC) is a newer insurance product in the U.S. that is more private in Europe. The policy is generally purchased to insure a company's existing accounts receivables against losses that might result from its customers' bankruptcy, slow pay, or default. Historically, these insurance policies have been widely used to facilitate international trade deals, and by government, export credit agencies to ensure the seller against buyer default. However, this insurance product is now also commonly used to ensure a company's domestic receivables. To pursue a claim, the business must follow the due diligence requirements on all new clients for whom credit is offered as prescribed by the insurance company.

While this insurance policy is likely not relevant to most small businesses, if the small business commonly sells to foreign parties, a trade credit insurance policy may exist. To verify if a trade credit policy exists, the business owner should review their outstanding foreign sales contracts to determine if the buyer had a duty to purchase a policy as a condition of the sale.

Directors and Officers Insurance

Directors and Officers Insurance (D&O) policies are purchased by a company to protect its officers and directors against suits from shareholders or other parties. The policy only covers the actions of officers or directors in the performance of their duties to the company.

There are three different types of D&O insurance:

1. Side A insurance covers the cost of an officer or director's legal expense. This policy will also provide funds to the officer or director if the company is financially unable to.
2. Side B coverage reimburses the corporation for the legal expenses it incurs in protecting the officer or director.
3. Side C insurance covers the legal expense the corporation incurs in protecting their own interest.

Irrespective of the coverage, these policies usually have a monetary limitation, which can be adjusted when the policy is renewed.

As the coronavirus continues to spread, and the severity of the economic shock increases, public company officers and directors will be expected to take action. Officers and directors will be expected to keep the company in compliance with securities regulations and to protect shareholder value. Not attending to these issues could result in legal action from governmental entities and shareholders alike. Because these suits usually name officers and directors as defendants, they will initially look to the company to finance their legal defense.

Liquidity is a concern for Side B policyholders because the officer, director, or the company is expected to pay for the legal cost and be reimbursed later. During an economic shock, such policies might be of little value as all the parties involved may be illiquid and, therefore, unable to finance a proper defense.

The insurance policy relates to when the action occurred and not when the suit was commenced. So while the insurance company may attempt to reduce the amount of coverage, the reduction will only apply to the renewed policy's coverage period. This outbreak and the economic turmoil may persist for a few years. Therefore, the company should watch for possible policy limit reduction and premium increases.

Employment Practices Liability Insurance

Employment Practices Liability Insurance (EPL) is an insurance policy that is intended to cover wrongful acts that occur in the management of employees. EPL insurance is generally sold as part of a management liability package that also includes the D&O insurance discussed above. Typically, these policies cover events related to wrongful termination, inappropriate workplace conduct, and defamation. However, the policy does not cover intentional or fraudulent acts. The policy protects officers, directors, managers, and employees of the company. In some cases, the policy will cover the cost of legal defense but reduce the policy limit coverage in the process. As already discussed, during times of economic shock, businesses will have to quickly make staffing adjustments to protect the business and its future. Some adversely affected employees may retaliate by taking actions based on prior grievances, wrongful termination, or discrimination based on race, sex, or disability. As a result, the business owner should review its management liability policy to ensure EPL insurance is included.

Commercial Umbrella Liability Insurance

Commercial Umbrella Liability Insurance policies are intended to provide an extra layer of protection by covering losses that exceed other underlying insurance policy limits. Commercial umbrella insurance policies may extend coverage beyond the underlying insurance policies.

Additionally, some umbrella policies have separate exclusions that might result in a slight mismatch between underlying policy coverage and what the umbrella policy will address. Some umbrella policies specifically exclude claims due to illness, plagues, or viruses. Therefore, the business owner should review the terms of their umbrella policy carefully.

State Insurance Legislation Activity

As this outbreak continues to cause economic turmoil, some states have stepped in to prevent insurance companies from taking actions detrimental to their clients. Some states are attempting to pass legislation to preventing insurance companies from canceling any commercial policies, including business income and business interruption policies. Other states have proposed legislation requiring insurance companies to cover COVID-19 related business interruption insurance claims irrespective of policy language to the contrary. These proposed statues would apply to businesses with less than 100 or 150 employees (depending on the state) and would be retroactive to early March. Many of the proposed statutes are retroactive to early March. States are offering to reimburse insurance companies for the additional insurance payouts. If state legislatures successfully pass these bills, the legislation will likely fail constitutional review under the Takings Clause. Further, it is unclear if the insurance companies have the capital to facilitate these payments and wait for reimbursements. When reviewing your insurance policy, it is essential to examine recent state insurance legislation as they may modify the terms in your policy.

Making a Claim

The good news is that most insurance claims are quickly and fairly resolved, but if the insurance company attempts to delay payment or dispute the amount recoverable, it may be advisable to seek the advice of an insurance attorney.

If the business owner believes they have a legitimate insurance claim, they should take steps to preserve their rights by timely filing a notice of loss within the policy terms. For business owners that have policies approaching expiration, filing a notice of circumstances before the policy expires will preserve the coverage even if a renewed policy expressly excludes COVID-19 related claims. These notices should be carefully worded to ensure the communication of specific facts with no room for misinterpretation.

When making a claim related to the closure of a business or a significant loss, insurance companies know that the policyholder will be in a vulnerable position. Under these circumstances, it is common for some insurance companies to attempt to exploit the policyholder by delaying or reducing the policy payout. It is common for legal action related to insurance claims to continue for years after a natural disaster. In some cases, policyholders may be able to pursue a claim of bad faith against insurance companies when they intentionally underpay or deny claims. Some states include failure to timely pay or investigate a claim as an act of bad faith. Therefore, the business owner should document their cooperation with insurance company requests in case the insurance company attempts to unreasonably delay payment, and litigation is needed.

Finally, some states consider misrepresentation of a policy's provisions by the insurance company or one of its agents as an act of bad faith. So the business owner should also review all email and written correspondence with the insurances and brokers to verify the coverage requested is what insurance company purported to provide.

CHAPTER SIX

CONTRACTS

Contracts are everywhere, and most people enter contracts all the time without realizing one was ever formed. In business, contracts take on a different level of importance because these contracts are typically created purposefully and are relied on to ensure the health and success of the business. In times of emergency or economic upheaval, it is common for businesses to be unable to perform their obligations under a contract. While the effects of such breach may be minor to the breaching party, other parties who rely on the goods or services under the contract may be materially and irrevocably harmed.

Most contract disputes are settled informally through open discussion between the parties. Usually, parties don't even consider the issues a "contract dispute", but rather an ongoing relationship between the parties. Typically, the thought of taking legal action is not considered because the injury suffered is not worth the time to litigate, and legal action may have negative consequences in the local business community. Open discussion is preferable because businesses can, and routinely do make mistakes that reasonable parties can come together and resolve. However, in emergency situations, some parties may not be reasonable and negotiations will not be a viable option.

As a result, it is beneficial for the small business owner to have a basic understanding of what a contract is and the circumstances under which they may be breached. While we discuss some basic contract law concepts, we believe pragmatic actions that benefit the company should be preferred over legal action, which can take months or years to resolve. The threat of legal action can have a chilling effect on both parties. Therefore, irrespective of the legal wrong suffered, ignoring minor issues to navigate the current circumstances may be the best approach. Please note the following is a general discussion of contracts. Contract law analysis is fact-driven, and state laws may vary. Therefore, business owners should seek counsel if a contract dispute arises that cannot be resolved between the parties.

First, contracts for goods are treated differently, then contracts for the provision of services. The common law controls contracts for services in most states. Common law is a body of law based on historic legal rulings that have been developed by the courts in a particular state over the years. Conversely, contracts for the sale of goods are generally covered under the Uniform Commercial Code (UCC), which most states have adopted to varying degrees. So, knowing the type of contract involved is critical to addressing specific issues that arise.

Generally, contracts for the provision of services that could take less than a year to perform do not need to be in writing. While most professional service agreements are memorialized through a writing, it is common for the parties to forgo written documentation of changes to their agreement over time. As a result, parties may have an agreement many years after an original contract is signed with a different scope of services and pricing. In these situations, one party may want to point to the original contract to pay a different price or provide a different level of service. However, courts can look at the historical interactions and courses of dealing between the parties and decide to resolve a contract dispute on those interactions instead of the contract as written. Therefore, it is essential to understand that the written document, if it exists, may only be the starting point in your understanding of what the actual agreement between you and the other party is. What follows is a brief discussion on the common types of defenses to performance under contracts: impossibility, impracticability, force majeure, and frustration of purpose.

Impossibility

In times of natural disasters or emergencies that make it impossible for a company to perform its duties under a contract, the company may be able to claim a defense of impossibility. Impossibility can arise due to the death or incapacity of a party who was to provide personal services under the contract. The destruction of property that was the focus of the contract may also deem performance impossible and be a defense for the breaching party. Additionally, the acts to be performed under the contract may become illegal after the contract was formed, thus making it impossible for a performing party to comply with their obligations. For instance, if a party has a contract with a restaurant to host a gathering, and the state declares that all restaurants are to close except for delivery and to-go orders (as has been the case in most states), the restaurant would not be liable for breaching the contract, as performance would now be illegal.

As this viral outbreak has affected the Chinese global supply chains, it is likely that some suppliers will, in fact, not be able to deliver the goods specified in the contract at the time needed. As with the above example, impossibility may be a defense as the supply disruption was due to the Chinese government implementing a quarantine that prevented companies from fulfilling their obligations.

As China resumes manufacturing and exporting to businesses, suppliers may attempt to excuse their delivery of goods because of price fluctuations or may attempt to significantly increase prices based on the business's needs or scarcity of the goods. Unfortunately, price fluctuations do not result in a defense to the performance of a contract. It has long been held that changes in price are foreseeable risks that parties can mitigate. Under such a breach, the non-breaching party could find another supplier in the open market and purchase the needed goods at the prevailing market price. The purchaser could then pursue legal action against the breaching party for damages based on the difference between the price the parties agreed upon and the price the non-breaching party paid.

The inverse of the above example is also a possibility, as pricing for goods and services may decrease during the following months as companies face high levels of competition to retain existing clients and acquire new ones. Here, an existing customer may attempt to breach a contract with the business after they have found better offers through a competitor. As long as the company can perform the agreed-upon services or deliver the goods in question, the customer would be unable to exit the contract based on price alone. Under such circumstances, the business could pursue the lost profit on the contract. If the contract is for goods, courts could add the additional cost of storing and transporting goods that should have been delivered to the customer.

Impracticability

Impracticability allows parties to avoid performance under a contract when an item or event, which was an underlying assumption of the agreement, does not come into existence. Impracticability must make performance extremely expensive and/or significantly more difficult with neither party being able to anticipate the failure of the assumption. For example, a conditional event could be relevant when it prevents a party from acquiring the supplies needed to perform its obligations. Companies may also have a defense when the death or incapacity of a particular person makes the performance impracticable. To determine if a specific person was necessary to perform a contract, one test is to ask if the incapacitated person could have delegated the obligation to another. However, it is essential to note that a change in price alone is not sufficient to trigger the defense of impracticability.

UCC contracts for the sale of goods are treated slightly differently. UCC Sec. 2–615, note four, explicitly states that changes in markets that result in an increase or decrease in price by themselves are insufficient to trigger impracticability. However, note 4 goes on to state that, among other things, war, crop failures, or failures of significant suppliers that result in a market change or prevent the party from acquiring the needed inventory could qualify as impracticability. As we have previously discussed, the coronavirus outbreak has affected global supply chains and companies' abilities to purchase necessary products. Therefore, this defense may be available to some companies who have been affected by the supply chain disruption.

Frustration of Purpose

Also known as commercial frustration, the defense of frustration of purpose may be available when the original purpose for entering into a contract is no longer viable. This defense requires that the purpose or event for which the contract was made must be the underlying assumption of the contract. Neither party entering into the contract could have anticipated at the time of forming the agreement that a particular event or condition would occur (or not occur). Further, this defense requires neither party assumed any risk as a result of the occurrence or non-occurrence of the event.

In the context of the coronavirus, contracting parties could not have anticipated upon inception that this pandemic would occur, virtually obliterating the entire purpose for the agreement. The purposes for contracting by a business may have been affected so substantially that the contract is essentially no longer needed. As a result, contracts may be voided due to the coronavirus. For example, a contract with a piano player to help create ambiance and enhance a restaurant patron's experience may be voided as eat-in services are currently illegal, making the purpose for the piano player unnecessary. As with other topics discussed in this book, the availability of this contract defense is based on the facts and circumstances involved. The business owner should consult with an attorney before taking any action detrimental to a contract.

Mitigating Damages

When a contract is breached, the non-breaching party has a duty to mitigate the damages. To do this, the non-breaching party must take reasonable steps to limit their losses. As already discussed, reasonableness is based on the facts and circumstances involved in a given situation. For instance, many businesses may be dissolving over the next few months. In the process, they will likely breach long-term commercial lease agreements with their landlords. In most states, the landlord must make reasonable attempts to find a new tenant to limit damages. Similarly, restaurants may have a defense to paying rent during the outbreak under the theories of impossibility, impracticability, and frustration of purpose because it is illegal to use the facilities as a restaurant. However, before breaching the lease, the restaurant owner should reasonably attempt to make profitable use of the facilities before breaching the lease agreement.

Contract Modification

Contract modification occurs when the parties to a contract mutually agree to alter some of the terms of the agreement. The modification can be related to the agreement to buy or sell goods, contract services or employment contracts. In most situations, these modifications are honored by the parties without issue. However, in some situations, one of the parties may try to find a way out of the modified contract. Knowing a few general rules about contract modification can be helpful if the circumstances require the parties to change the terms of an agreement.

As discussed above, contracts are treated differently under common law and UCC. Under common law, an attempt to modify a contract must also include new consideration. To modify an agreement for services, terms of payment, or changed contractual obligations, new bargained-for exchange (consideration) must be present, different from that previously agreed. However, if a party changes their position to their detriment in reliance on a contract modification that is not supported by consideration, the court may still enforce the modified contract in the interest of justice.

Under the UCC, the parties can modify an existing contract without the need to provide new consideration. However, the court does require an element of good faith. Under the current coronavirus outbreak, one party attempting to take advantage of the emergency and raising prices on the other party would not be considered an act in good faith. Therefore, courts could void the modification and reestablish the original terms of the contract.

Force Majeure Clauses

Force majeure allows a party to a contract to be excused when an "act of God" or some other unforeseen, extraordinary event occurs that prevents one of the party's from performing their obligations under the contract. To be applicable, the agreement must contain a force majeure clause that releases the party to the contract under such circumstances. Additionally, courts will also look to see if the event was genuinely unforeseeable and if performance under the contract was made impossible as a result of the "act of God." Each state has various requirements for what is needed to trigger the force majeure clause. As a rule, most courts treat force majeure clauses narrowly based on the specific language of the provision. Additionally, some states require the "act of God" to be unforeseeable, while others simply require an extraordinary event. For instance, some states may not view hurricanes as an unforeseen "act of God" if they are common to the regions in which the parties are to perform the service.

Currently, there is a lot of attention being paid to this contract element as people examine their contract language to see if a force majeure clause exists and if the COVID-19 outbreak could qualify as an unforeseeable act of God. Even if this element is satisfied, the party breaching the contract would still have to prove that the extraordinary events have actually made their performance impossible. As with the defense of impracticability, (discussed above), the mere fact that performance has become more difficult or financially costly does not qualify as an extraordinary event to trigger the force majeure clause. However, some states have allowed force majeure when performance has only become impracticable but not necessarily impossible. Remember that the specific language of the clause could change the general standards outlined above. Therefore, it is advisable to engage an attorney that specializes in contract law to verify what options are available, and what a specific state's requirements are.

The Next Step

Armed with this knowledge, it is wise for the business owner to find all critical contracts between their company and their suppliers and customers. Review the language of the contracts to see if there are any provisions related to a party's rights to terminate the agreement. Additionally, the business owner should also be aware of changes in state contract law and the treatment of force majeure events. Follow this review with an examination of state and federal actions taken during the outbreak, and what reasonably foreseeable future actions the state or federal government may take. Then ask yourself if those actions could result in any of your key contracts becoming impossible to perform or whether they qualify as a force majeure event.

Consider the following:

- Will your customers' and suppliers' ability to perform their obligations under the contract?

- Will your clients still need, or even be in business, to purchase the goods or services you provide?

- Will your suppliers be in business to sell the supplies, inventory, or service that your company needs within the coming months?

Once you have assessed the potential effects of government actions on your contract, and the probability of your clients and suppliers being able to continue the contracts, analyze the consequences of a possible contract breach on your business. In conjunction with this step, also consider the alternative suppliers and service providers that might be available to fulfill the company's requirements if a breach occurs. This may require opening a dialog with your supplier's competitor to get a better understanding of their lead times and pricing. But, be warned that such actions could harm your existing relationship with your suppliers if they learn that you are considering other suppliers during this fragile economic period. In this process, the business owner may find that there are cheaper and more stable sources for needed goods and services in the market. To the extent that a supplier contract allows the company to exit the agreement, the business owner should consider doing so if a cheaper, more stable source exists.

Finally, be proactive. If you notice issues with your suppliers and customers, open a line of communication with them to see what their current situation is so that you can get a better idea of what their future viability might be. Also, understand that other suppliers and customers will also likely be going through the same financial troubles as the suppliers and customers you already have. Therefore, be careful not to sign new contracts with customers or suppliers who might themselves be unable to fulfill their contractual obligations.

CHAPTER SEVEN

BANKRUPTCY AND DEBT RESTRUCTURING

Running a small business is a full-contact sport in which the odds are stacked against the business owner. According to the Small Business Administration (SBA), about half of all new businesses are out of business within 12 to 18 months. Generally, the main reason for failure in the early stages is due to underfunding. Most new companies typically do not become profitable, if at all, until their second or third year. After a natural disaster, these "newer" businesses have a higher risk of failure because they are not profitable, still developing a customer base, and will have difficulty proving the economic injury needed to get an SBA loan.

According to a survey of 1,500 small businesses who are Goldman Sachs 10,000 Small Business participants, 51% of the respondents reported that they would only be able to continue operations for less than three months. According to Merchant Maverick, it takes the SBA roughly 4 to 5 weeks to approve and fund an SBA disaster loan. Therefore, a lot of companies may not have the liquidity to continue to operate while they wait for the 4 to 5 weeks to get funding from the SBA.

History

An increase in bankruptcies after a severe economic shock is expected. Understanding the timing and relationship between events and resulting bankruptcies is vital for business owners to make informed decisions about who to give credit to and when.

The current coronavirus outbreak and the related economic shock will likely result in many companies having to file bankruptcy. While most small business owners have a general understanding of what bankruptcy is, having a better functional understanding of the different kinds of bankruptcies is essential. It is likely many businesses will have clients who are forced into filing some form of bankruptcy in the coming years. As an example, it is helpful to look at the effects of the Severe Acute Respiratory Syndrome (SARS) outbreak, which occurred in 2002 and 2003. NBC News estimated that the SARS outbreak resulted in worldwide economic losses of about $40 billion due to the disruptions in international supply chains and suspension of business activities, predominantly in Asia.

SARS effects on bankruptcy filings in the three years after the outbreak were significant and clearly visible. When examining total bankruptcies filed by year for the three years immediately after the SARS outbreak, bankruptcies increased significantly between 2003 to 2005. The average bankruptcy filings between 1999 to 2001 was 1,289,546, as opposed to the 1,606,136 filed from 2003 to 2005, a 25% increase. To put the data in perspective, the U.S. economy was still recovering from the economic shock related to the September 11, 2001, terrorist attacks. Therefore, some companies were already in a precarious economic predicament before the SARS outbreak. By contrast, at the beginning of the Coronavirus outbreak, the U.S. economy was close to full employment with stock market prices at historic highs. So, the initial assessment would seem to indicate that the potential expected effect of this outbreak on bankruptcy filings in the next two years would be less dramatic. However, as of the writing of this book, CCN.com is estimating the potential economic damage related to the Coronavirus to come in around $2.7 trillion based on the number of worldwide infections multiplied by the financial loss per person during the

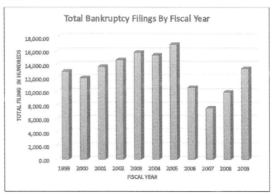

Source: Administrative Office of the U.S. Courts

SARS outbreak. In an interview with CNBC, Ray Dalio estimated corporate losses in the U.S. alone to be over $4 trillion, which is significantly larger than the damages caused by the SARS outbreak in 2002 – 2003. According to Forbes, the U.S. stock market losses alone resulted in an economic loss of roughly $4.6 trillion. Therefore, it is expected that the effect of this outbreak on bankruptcy filings over the next few years will be significantly more substantial than the SARs outbreak of 2003.

To better prepare the small business owner for the effects of their clients filing bankruptcy, or if the business owner decides that bankruptcy is a potential option for their company, we offer the following general information.

Automatic Stay

When petitioners file bankruptcy, they receive an automatic stay. The stay protects the bankrupt party from foreclosures, garnishments, collection lawsuits, and other legal asset-seizure actions. Any current collection actions are placed on hold at the commencement of the bankruptcy filing. Further collection or legal actions are automatically suspended. The automatic stay exists irrespective of the form of bankruptcy. Therefore, the bankruptcy stay can be used to protect assets and delay creditors from taking legal steps against the business or its owner. Filing bankruptcy can buy the business owner and the company the time needed to become stable.

Chapter 13 Debt Adjustment

Chapter 13 bankruptcy is used for individuals attempting to reorganize their debts. It can also be used for sole proprietors as the business is not legally distinguishable from the individual owner. In this form of bankruptcy, the small business/individual attempts to reorganize their debts by asking the court to authorize a payment plan different than the ones the debtor initially made. Once filed and approved by the court, the small business owner will make the scheduled payments for the period prescribed. After the payment plan has been completed, any remaining debts left unpaid are to be written off by the creditor.

While a well-planned bankruptcy payment plan does increase the chance the small business will survive, historically, most individuals and companies falter on the program during the repayment period. Therefore, using a Chapter 13 bankruptcy should be approached with caution as it is a longterm commitment.

Chapter 11 Business Reorganization

Chapter 11 bankruptcy is a reorganization form of bankruptcy typically used for larger businesses. Generally, this form of bankruptcy is used by partnerships and corporations with a viable financial future and sole proprietors whose income exceeds the maximum to qualify for a Chapter 13 bankruptcy.

Under Chapter 11 bankruptcy, the company will continue in operation under the supervision of a court-appointed trustee. As part of the bankruptcy, the company will file a payment plan similar to a Chapter 13, but the creditors of the company get to decide if they want to accept the plan through a majority vote. The court will also need to approve the plan to ensure the creditor's committee does not mistreat minority creditor voting interests. As part of the plan, the company can terminate contracts and leases, reclaim assets, pay a portion of outstanding debt, and discharge the rest.

Chapter 11 reorganizations are not always successful. These bankruptcies can be complex, and it may take years to get a viable plan approved by all the appropriate stakeholders. Historically, about 75% of all businesses that file for Chapter 11 reorganizations are unsuccessful in complying with the approved bankruptcy plan. Ultimately they end up filing Chapter 7 liquidation bankruptcy within a matter of years.

Chapter 7 Liquidation

Chapter 7 bankruptcy is used by businesses to cease operations and liquidate assets systematically. The money received from liquidation is used to pay off creditors and bondholders with the remainder, if any, going to shareholders depending on the classes of stock. To be successful in a Chapter 7 bankruptcy, the applicant must pass a means test. If the applicant's income exceeds a predetermined amount, they will not be allowed to file a Chapter 7 bankruptcy.

If approved, the court will appoint a trustee to take possession of the business and its assets. The trustee is tasked with dissolving the company, finding and documenting all potential assets, selling the business assets, and then distributing the money to the appropriate parties. In some cases, the trustee may decide that the business is worth more intact and attempt to sell the company to new owners. At the end of the process, the business owner is released from any remaining debt obligations. However, partnerships and corporations are not issued discharges.

Chapter 7 bankruptcy is generally the right choice for businesses that have no future financial viability. For instance, a company that cannot maintain the extra debt that it might have to incur to ride out the current outbreak may decide a better course of action is to liquidate the company and seek other opportunities.

Small Business Reorganization Act

The Small Business Reorganization Act (SBRA) was passed in August 2019 and went into effect on February 20, 2020. The act attempts to streamline the complex Chapter 11 repayment plan approval process and reduce legal expenses. It applies to small businesses with debts of less than $2,725,625. However, the act excludes debts owed to affiliates with 50% or more of the obligations arising from the commercial or business activities of the debtor. The CARE Act temporarily increased the debt limit to $7.5 million for cases filed before March 27, 2021, at which time the threshold will return to $2,725,625. The SBRA does not apply to those owning a company that consists of a single piece of real estate.

The SBRA does not require an unsecured creditors committee unless the court so requires. Additionally, the courts have greater leeway to confirm a plan without the approval of the impaired debtors, (cramdown) and even allows the court to dispense with some debtor priority rules.

Finally, while the court appoints a trustee, the debtor remains in possession of the business and operates the business. Additionally, the debtor is given the same power as the trustee. However, the court can remove the debtor's ability to control and possess the assets in cases of fraud, incompetence, or dishonesty that occurred before or after the case is filed.

The SBRA only applies to an eligible chapter 11 bankruptcy at the debtor's request.

Bankruptcy Preferential Payments – Claw Backs

Preferential payments to creditors

Preferred payments are payments or transfers of property made by a debtor to an unsecured creditor with an aggregate value over $600 within 90 days of the debtor filing bankruptcy. The payments are assumed to be preferential because it is presumed that the debtor was bankrupt 90 days before the filing. As discussed above, one of the trustee's duties is to find all property that can be used to pay back the debtor's creditors. To that end, it is standard practice for trustees to take legal steps to attempt to "clawback" or reacquire payments made to creditors within 90 days of the debtor's filing bankruptcy.

This can be especially difficult for small businesses for whom the debtor was a large client. In these situations, the small business may have been waited months to get paid on outstanding invoices. Most of the time, the business owner uses the monies to pay off their debts, which are likely also late due to their client's slow pay. As a result, it is common for these clawback actions to put the small business in significant financial stress or cause that small business to file bankruptcy.

In preferential payment claims, it is the responsibility of the company to prove that the clawback provisions do not apply to them. There are various ways that the business may be able to do so. While we will cover a few of the methods here as a general overview, the company should seek counsel from a bankruptcy attorney.

First, preferential payments only apply to unsecured creditors. Therefore, if the transaction in question were related to a cash transaction, then the payment would not be applicable for clawback.

Along the same lines, if the payment of the existing debt was coupled with other valuable considerations, the courts generally will not void the payment. Examples include an agreement to ship goods currently on hold or services potentially not to be performed as a result of the debtor's past-due account. Here if the creditor provides the goods or services based on the promise of the creditor to make a payment on the past-due account, the promise acts as consideration and can be a defense to the trustee's clawback attempt.

Second, the courts generally will not make an order to void a payment when the creditor did not know or have reasonable grounds to know that the debtor was insolvent.

A similar argument can be made if the small business creditor entered the transaction with the debtor in good faith. However, these defenses are the hardest to prove to the courts.

Finally, the creditor may be able to avoid the clawback attempt by showing that the payments were part of a continual pattern of an existing business relationship. Here the small business has to prove the payments received were in line with the historical course of dealing, and payment patterns had not changed recently.

Preferential payments to family and friends

When a debtor transfers assets to a family member or friend before the bankruptcy, those payments are subject to clawback. Unlike preferential payment claims to creditors, the trustee can look one year back to reclaim payments to family and friends. While some business owners have purposefully delayed bankruptcy to try to get outside the statute of limitations, such acts are considered fraudulent, and the court can take steps to extend the statute of limitations in the interest of justice.

Workout Agreements

Workout agreements are negotiated agreements between the lender and the borrower to adjust the terms of a loan currently in default. Workout agreements help avoid bankruptcy or foreclosure, resulting in a better outcome for both lender and the borrower. After a workout negotiation, the terms of the existing loan are adjusted based on the borrower's financial abilities, and the loan is removed from default status. These non-bankruptcy arrangements are suitable for the borrower because they can avoid the stigma, cost, and stress of bankruptcy while achieving a similar outcome.

Lenders only approve workout agreements if it results in a better return than they would receive in bankruptcy. However, lenders are not generally under any obligation to restructure an existing loan, and some lenders do not entertain workout requests.

The parties can adjust various terms of a loan to achieve the desired outcome. Common loan modifications include:

1. Lowering the interest rate of the loan to make the monthly payments more affordable.

2. Extending the term of the loan to lower the monthly payments.

3. Payment forbearance or pausing repayment requirements for a period to allow the borrower to find their financial footing. These missed payments can be made up at the end of the forbearance period, and in some instances, the lender may temporarily suspend interest charges.

4. Payment deferment allows the borrower to miss some loan payments and make up those missed payments at the end of the loan, in effect

extending the payment period by the payments missed. While interest generally runs during this period in some cases, banks will temporarily suspend the interest charges.

It is important to note that forbearance is not deferment. Forbearance requires the missed payments to be paid at the end of the forbearance period, and deferment adds payments to the end of the loan to make up the difference. This distinction is especially important for real estate investors who are using the CARES Act federal mortgage forbearance option to delay mortgage payments.

The CARES Act prevents mortgage companies from reporting creditors who were current before a forbearance request as delinquent while in the forbearance period. However, mortgage companies are placing notes on the debtor's credit reports stating the account is in forbearance status. The credit reporting agencies are using those notes to drop participant's credit scores significantly. This will make refinancing and acquisition of new credit or loans difficult in the near future.

5. Forgiving a portion of the principal loan balance to reduce the monthly payments.

Some loan adjustments may trigger a taxable event. The IRS treats canceled debt as income to the borrower and taxes it accordingly. Therefore, the borrower should consult a CPA or tax attorney before negotiating a workout agreement to understand their options and the potential tax effects. For pass-through entities like partnerships, LLCs and S-Corps, canceled debt income will flow down to the partner's, member's or shareholder's income K-1. The owners will be personally responsible for the tax liability.

Workout negotiations have a higher chance of success when an experienced financial professional or attorney is engaged. These professionals will have a better idea of what the creditor would receive in bankruptcy and therefore know what terms might be acceptable to the lender while achieving the borrower's goals.

CHAPTER EIGHT
NONPROFITS

Nonprofits and charitable organizations play an essential part in the recovery of communities after natural disasters and economic shocks. After an emergency, it is common for nonprofits and charitable religious and community organizations to step in to offer aid, comfort, and organize local responses to those in need. Because of their organic nature and localized knowledge, most nonprofits can quickly respond to events in ways that governments and businesses cannot.

However, nonprofits and charitable organizations are also subject to the same economic forces that have been discussed throughout this book. Unlike businesses, most smaller nonprofits do not have the business, marketing, and legal resources to assist them through economic stresses they may encounter. Therefore, we have included a chapter dedicated exclusively to nonprofits, to arm them with knowledge the organization and their boards of directors and managers need to chart a course through this outbreak.

The good news is the previous discussions in chapter two on leadership, marketing, and spending are all applicable to nonprofits and charities. In some ways, leadership under the current circumstances is easier than in for-profit companies. While some for-profit companies provide valuable goods and services to the market that genuinely make people's lives better, many companies have profit as their primary goal. The employees who work for these companies may still find joy in the work they do, but the motivation that emanates from purpose does not exist. By contrast, at their core, nonprofits exist to serve a purpose and help others. The employees who work for nonprofits and charitable organizations are generally driven by something more than a paycheck. In uncertain times, this sense of purpose can be developed in a way that may be difficult for other companies. Therefore, leadership should connect their messages to the core mission of the nonprofit and demonstrate how the activities of the organization play a part in the fight against the outbreak.

As mentioned in Chapter 2, controlling the narrative is imperative from a marketing perspective. Instead of messaging focused around COVID-19, the marketing message should focus on the nonprofit's core mission, and how its programs meet the immediate needs of the community. Resources should be channeled in ways that make an impact. These activities can be leveraged using traditional and social media to strengthen donor and community support. But such activities will be harder to execute and capture because of social distancing requirements. Therefore, nonprofits will have to tell their story in new ways as the traditional image of volunteers serving food to the hungry or providing blankets to the homeless is not available at the moment.

Collaboration

Unlike for-profit businesses, nonprofits tend to be less competitive and, therefore, more likely to collaborate with other for-profit and nonprofit organizations with similar or complementary missions. Such collective activity leads to a more efficient use of scarce resources and a wider marketing reach. Organizations that might have been unwilling to participate in collaborative endeavors may now be open to such opportunities. While collaborations may result in more benefits to the target community, such activity could have longer-term benefits due to the transfer of knowledge and processes that will naturally occur during these joint activities. Additionally, the development of a strong supportive relationship within the nonprofit community will lead to a more stable community support structure over time.

Finance

The main difference between for-profit businesses and nonprofits is nonprofits generally do not pursue revenue but rather operate through charitable donations, grants, and some limited for-profit activity. To the extent that grants are related to state and local funding sources, the nonprofit needs to be in close contact with the source to verify the stability of the grant. Currently, states and cities are spending a significant amount on the COVID-19 response. While the federal government is taking some steps to provide financial assistance to state and local entities, many agencies will likely find their resources significantly depleted as a result of their efforts. They may not have the funds to continue offering grants.

Similarly, those donors who historically support nonprofits may find themselves in financial stress due to losses on investments, suspension of their business, or the loss/uncertainty of their continued employment. Spring and summer fundraisers traditionally used to support charitable organizations have also been canceled or are now in doubt due to mandated social distancing rules. Therefore, communication with internal and external stakeholders is of utmost importance during these challenging times to maintain donor support.

Because of this dependency on grants and donations, the planning and management of cash flow to a nonprofit are of vital concern. Usually, nonprofits do not have a significant cash reserve to get them through rough times. As a result, nonprofits who experience substantial decreases in donations and grants must quickly cut expenses to avoid a negative bank balance. This means the officers and directors of the nonprofit must manage costs proactively and investigate any expense overruns to see if those expense variances will be recurring. If the expense is recurring at an elevated level, then other adjustments will have to be made to eliminate the cash drain. This might mean reducing expenses in another cost category or finding a new, cheaper supplier.

To assist with potential disruption in charitable giving, the CARE Act increased the deduction limit for corporations from 10% to 25% of the corporation's adjusted gross income. The act also increased the deduction limitation on food inventory from 15% to 25%. In the 2020 tax year, the CARE Act now allows individuals who make a cash donation to use the deduction for up to 100% of their adjusted gross income if the taxpayer itemizes their deductions. For those taxpayers who do not itemize, the CARE Act allows a $300 per taxpayer, charitable deduction, for cash gifts to public charities. Additionally, while the CARE Act waived required minimum retirement account distributions, the act did not suspend qualified charitable distributions.

Nonprofits can use the new tax laws to incentivize current and prospective donors to donate and benefit from the enhanced tax deductions. Along the same lines, because taxpayers are not required to take retirement distributions in 2020, they may be more inclined to make charitable distributions from their retirement account to help nonprofits in their local community.

For donation shortfalls, nonprofit organizations can pursue an SBA loan. Under the Economic Injury loan discussed previously, the SBA offers loans to charitable organizations with a 30-year repayment period at an interest rate of 2.75%. Additionally, the CARE Act SBA loans discussed in Chapter 3, are also available to nonprofit, veterans, and tribal organizations with 500 or fewer employees. This means that nonprofit organizations can also apply for an SBA loan advance for up to $10,000.

Payroll Protection Program

As discussed in Chapter 3, the government will provide a loan that, if used in the prescribed manner, will be converted into a grant and forgiven after a period of time. This program is also available to nonprofits in operation since February 15, 2020, with less than 500 employees, who have been harmed as a result of the outbreak. Because the program is managed through the SBA 7(a) loan option, the nonprofit will need to contact their banker to apply. The headcount and payroll reduction restrictions are applicable, as well. Unlike the Economic Injury loans that discounted the interest rate to nonprofits, the Payroll Protection Program's interest rate remains at 1% for nonprofits.

If the directors of a nonprofit believe that a loan is not the right solution, the SBA has other resources for nonprofits and charitable organizations on their website. Other major corporations also have various programs to help nonprofits. For instance, Microsoft has a program to support nonprofits in their mission by providing the software necessary to allow nonprofit employees to work from home.

Employment Issues

As discussed in Chapter 4, the organization has a duty to protect its employees. Nonprofits may find this duty difficult to comply with if the work requires direct interaction with the public. Here added requirements for personal protective gear might be in order. The increased cost of these added measures may make finding alternative methods of delivering the goods or services economically necessary. As already discussed above, this may require the nonprofit to collaborate with other nonprofits and larger corporations to develop solutions.

Self-Insured Nonprofits Relief

Government and nonprofit entities have the choice to either pay unemployment to the state or treated as a reimbursable employer. Generally, nonprofits choose to pay unemployment insurance as part of their payroll expense. For those nonprofits that choose to reimburse the state for benefits paid to dismissed employees, the CARE Act provides nonprofit organizations with reimbursement for half the amounts paid to the state's unemployment trust fund for the period of March 13, 2020, to December 31, 2020.

Board of Directors

As discussed in Chapter 5, one of the insurance policies that a business may have is a D&O insurance policy to protect their officers and directors from legal issues that might arise in the performance of their duties. These same issues exist for those who sit on the boards of nonprofits as well. Under the current circumstances, nonprofit directors are expected to be informed of the existing operational and financial health of the charitable organization and follow formalities when taking actions in response to the issues that come before the board of directors. The directors also have a duty to oversee the officers of the nonprofit organization. Under the current circumstances, it is foreseeable that some directors may be preoccupied with other issues and may not be able to devote the required amount of time needed to properly comply with their duties as a director of the nonprofit. The effects of a potential mistake could be devastating to the director and the nonprofit. Therefore, it is advisable that the nonprofit review their insurance policy to verify they have D&O insurance for their officers and directors before an actionable event occurs.

Bankruptcy

It is rare for nonprofits to file bankruptcy because, by their nature, spending is mostly dependent on donations and grants. As already discussed, the nonprofit's focus is strictly managing cash flow, which, as a general rule, means nothing is purchased in a nonprofit unless cash is already allocated for that transaction. Further, it is more difficult for nonprofits to qualify for loans than other businesses because providing support in communities does not directly result in profits to the charitable organization. But occasionally, nonprofits are faced with situations that require them to file bankruptcy.

While we have already covered bankruptcies in Chapter 7 of this book, there are a few subjects unique to nonprofit bankruptcies that should be addressed.

First, a nonprofit could potentially file a Chapter 7 liquidation or a Chapter 11 bankruptcy reorganization. The kind of bankruptcy chosen will depend on the nonprofit's ability to continue to generate cash through grants, contributions, and any other business endeavors coupled with assets the nonprofit has accumulated.

Second, the bankruptcy code restricts a nonprofit's ability to transfer assets after bankruptcy is filed, unlike for-profit businesses. Section 541(f) of the Bankruptcy Code states that nonprofits can only transfer assets to the same extent they could if they had not filed bankruptcy. So, while filing bankruptcy may protect nonprofit assets, it will not give the nonprofit a greater ability to transfer assets to another party.

Finally, bankruptcy issues are further complicated by potential restrictive language in donor grants. Often, large grants have language that restricts how the organization can use the assets. These grants may have contingency language in the original donation that revert the ownership of the assets to the grantor or another party at the occurrence of some future event, like bankruptcy. Further, some nonprofit assets may be harder to sell or transfer. Because nonprofits receive goods and services at significantly reduced prices, sales contracts generally include contractual or licensing agreements that limit the transfer of those assets to others. Therefore, nonprofits should review existing donations and grants agreements before filing bankruptcy or selling assets.

When nonprofits find themselves in financial hardship that could result in closure or bankruptcy, it is common for the nonprofit to find other nonprofits with complementary missions to whom they can sell or transfer their assets. By pursuing this strategy, nonprofits can ensure that their work and the assets they have collected continue to serve the purpose their donors intended while honoring the nonprofit's mission. Additionally, this strategy may also avoid some of the contracts and licensing restrictions previously discussed and potentially sidestep preexisting donor restrictions.

About the Authors

Phillip Zagotti, CPA, JD is a serial entrepreneur and partner at Zagotti & Burdette, CPA, where he focuses on tax, tax defense, forensics, mergers & acquisitions, and troubled company consulting. He regularly publishes articles through the firm's website and performs speaking engagements on tax and business issues.

Effrossini Simpson received her degree in history, and a master's in education before completing her law degree while raising her two children. She is passionate about her work with organizations concerned with fighting crime in the community and is an advocate for access to the justice system.

Mary Brannon is a corporate accounting and risk management professional. Her career spans over 20 years across multiple industries. She enjoys raising her entrepreneurial teenager and creating an encouraging space for her community to discuss financial literacy and achieve financial goals.

Thanks for reading! Please add a short review on Amazon and let us know what you thought!

Manufactured by Amazon.ca
Bolton, ON